THE CANTERBURY TALES

Geoffrey Chaucer

Prestwick House

LITERARY TOUCHSTONE CLASSICS

P.O. Box 658 Clayton, Delaware 19938 • www.prestwickhouse.com

SENIOR EDITOR: Paul Moliken

EDITORS: Darlene Gilmore

COVER DESIGN & PHOTOGRAPHY: Jen Mendoza
    Costume courtesy of Actors Attic
    Dover, Delaware • www.actorsattic.com

PRODUCTION: Jen Mendoza

Prestwick House
LITERARY TOUCHSTONE CLASSICS™

P.O. BOX 658 • CLAYTON, DELAWARE 19938
TEL: 1.800.932.4593
FAX: 1.888.718.9333
WEB: www.prestwickhouse.com

Prestwick House Teaching Units™, Activity Packs™, and Response Journals™ are the perfect complement for these editions. To purchase teaching resources for this book, visit www.prestwickhouse.com

This Prestwick House edition, is a selection of slightly modified tales as they originally appeared in Canterbury Tales: Rendered into Modern English by J. U. Nicolson, published in 1934 by Garden City Publishing Company, Inc., New York

ISBN 978-1-60843-935-5

THE CANTERBURY TALES

By Geoffrey Chaucer

CONTENTS

N OTES

The selected tales in this book have been translated into Modern English and reproduced in their entirety. As such, some of the content, dealing with themes of a sexual nature and including vulgar language, may not be appropriate for some classes. Teacher discretion is advised.

What is a literary classic and why are these classic works important to the world?

A literary classic is a work of the highest excellence that has something important to say about life and the human condition with great artistry. A classic, through its enduring presence, has withstood the test of time and is not bound by time, place, or customs. It speaks to us today as forcefully as it spoke to people one hundred or more years ago, and as forcefully as it will speak to people of future generations. For this reason, a classic is said to have universality.

G E O F F R E Y   C H A U C E R

GEOFFREY CHAUCER was born around 1343, in London. His father and grandfather were prosperous wine-traders. As a young man, Chaucer was able to gain a position in the court of a countess, and later, he became a valet in the court of King Edward III.

King Edward III, by unknown artist, late 16th century

In his teens, Chaucer served in the Hundred Years' War, and while in France, was taken prisoner and ransomed by the king himself.

Chaucer traveled to Italy, where he became familiar with the works of the great Italian poets Dante (1265-1321) and Boccaccio (1313-1375). He was also influenced by the French poets, whose works he translated.

Image of Chaucer as a pilgrim from Ellesmere Manuscript.

After his service in the court, Chaucer was given various mid-level positions in the government, including Comptroller of the Port of London. In this role, he oversaw customs regulations on incoming goods. He also traveled to Flanders (modern-day Holland and Belgium) on a government mission. All of these experiences influenced the *Canterbury Tales*.

Geoffrey Chaucer. 19th century image. From *The Illustrated Magazine of Art*. 1:1 (ca. 1853).

Another famous poem by Chaucer is *Troilus and Criseyde*, a love story of about 8,000 lines; he also wrote several shorter poetic works, authored a *Treatise on the Astrolabe* (an informative work about an important navigational tool used by sailors), and translated the late Roman philosopher Boethius' *Consolation of Philosophy* into English.

In the year 1400, Chaucer died of unknown causes; some scholars believe he was murdered by enemies of King Richard II. Though Europe was already undergoing tremendous change during his lifetime, Chaucer's death is often used as a marker of the end of the medieval period.

Reading Pointers for Sharper Insights

As you read *Canterbury Tales*, keep the following information in mind:

Historical Circumstances: In the fourteenth century, when Geoffrey Chaucer was writing, England was a savage place. War, plague, church scandal, and political controversy were all raging, and the author of the *Canterbury Tales* was in the middle of all of it.

The Hundred Years' War with France, which was actually a series of battles and not a continuous war, was in progress; Chaucer himself actually went to France as part of this war and was personally ransomed by King Edward III.

During the same time period, the Black Death, or bubonic plague, was devastating Europe. The chaos of the plague led to some dishonest behavior on the part of landowners, the clergy, and physicians but, more importantly, it permanently altered the order of European society. Whereas medieval society had generally been divided into three *estates* (clergy, aristocracy, and the freeman), the plague helped form a new category: the middle class. Since many workers died, there was a labor shortage; survivors, newly in demand, could lobby for higher wages and better working conditions. Eventually, their improvement in lifestyle became permanent.

The Peasants' Revolt of 1381 took place in response to a harsh tax on these laborers; Chaucer mentions one of the leaders of the Revolt, Jack Straw, in the *Nun's Priest's Tale*. As you read, notice how Chaucer both adheres to the idea of the three estates and departs from it. Which characters are easy to classify, and which seem to belong to more than one class?

The Catholic Church, by far the most important institution in Europe, was also experiencing internal strife. In 1378, a controversy over the papal election resulted in the naming of three popes, all of whom claimed legitimacy.

Within England, the theologian John Wycliffe was attacking the doctrine that priests must act as interpreters of God's word, and he asserted that each ordinary churchgoer had the power to understand God for himself. Wycliffe's followers, called *Lollards*, were attacked as heretics by the king, and several were beheaded. Can you find any hint of this religious violence in the *Canterbury Tales*?

Structure of the Church: The medieval church divided the clergy into two categories: *regular* and *secular*. The regular clergy were those men, like monks and friars, who belonged to a religious order and took vows of celibacy and poverty. Monks were supposed to live lives of quiet reflection, prayer and solitude, while friars were supposed to go out into their communities and help the people there. Friars were *mendicant*, which means that they owned no property and supported themselves on whatever money they were given by community members.

The secular clergy were men like the Parson; they were local priests and church officials who did not belong to any particular order.

In addition to these legitimate church employees, a number of other, less savory characters attached themselves to the Church to make money. Among these were *pardoners*, men who would dispense "pardon" from sin for a fee. *Summoners* call people to ecclesiastical (church) court, but for the right price, let the summons drop.

Finally, women had positions in the Church that mirrored those of some of the men; nuns, for instance, were the female equivalent of monks. However, unlike the monks, the nuns were not considered ordained clergy. The Prioress is an example of a high-ranking nun. How much does she have in common with the Monk and the Friar?

Economy: During the fourteenth century, Europe was gradually moving from an economy based on *feudalism* to a more open, money-based system. Under feudalism, society had been organized into different levels of lord and servant; at the bottom were the serfs, who owned no property and had no rights as citizens, and at the very top was the supreme lord, the king. This system dated from a time when Europe was primarily agricultural, and had relied on the trading of needed services—a serf, for example, would supply farm labor to his lord in return for housing and protection. Society was now becoming more *urbanized*, though, and its new economy was based on money and goods. The Knight, Squire, Yeoman, and Franklin, as well as the Reeve, are remnants of the old feudal system, while the Merchant, Five Guildsmen, and even the Wife of Bath reflect the emergence of the new system.

Of course, the transformation in Europe's economy was not as simple as an overnight conversion from feudalism to a money system; however, knowing that some of these changes were taking place, you can look for them in the *Canterbury Tales*.

Voice: Part of what makes the *Canterbury Tales* so complex is its multilayered structure. The narrator—who is not the same as Chaucer, the author—is retelling each pilgrim's story in that pilgrim's voice. Try to figure out who is really speaking: the author, the narrator, or the character. Is there ever a time when the character seems sincere, but the narrator or Chaucer is being ironic?

Language: You may be surprised at some of the words and images that Chaucer considered acceptable for literature. In fact, he himself, in the prologue to the Miller's Tale, apologizes for the obscenity he is "forced" to repeat. Why do you think he includes these kinds of stories?

Common Types of Story: Chaucer did not invent any of the stories he tells; he took the basic form of each from other sources. The Knight's Tale, for instance, is a typical story of *courtly love*—a romance in which a knight or gentleman goes to great lengths for a beautiful, seemingly unreachable woman. Tales that deliver a religious message or moral are based upon well-known fables and legends. What Chaucer does so creatively is to make these common stories say something about their teller. While we are reading about what happens in each tale, we are also sitting with the other pilgrims, watching the teller of the story and wondering about his or her own life.

The *General*

P R O L O G U E

WHEN APRIL with his showers sweet with fruit
The drought of March has pierced unto the root
And bathed each vein with liquor that has power
To generate therein and sire the flower;
5   When Zephyr[1] also has, with his sweet breath,
Quickened again, in every holt[2] and heath,
The tender shoots and buds, and the young sun
Into the Ram[3] one half his course has run,
And many little birds make melody
10 That sleep through all the night with open eye
(So Nature pricks them on to ramp and rage)—
Then do folk long to go on pilgrimage,[4]
And palmers[5] to go seeking out strange strands,[6]
To distant shrines well known in sundry[7] lands.
15 And specially from every shire's[8] end
Of England they to Canterbury wend,[9]
The holy blessed martyr[10] there to seek
Who helped them when they lay so ill and weak.
Befell that, in that season, on a day
20 In Southwark,[11] at the Tabard,[12] as I lay
Ready to start upon my pilgrimage
To Canterbury, full of devout courage,
There came at nightfall to that hostelry

[1] *the west wind*

[2] *wood*

[3] *the constellation Aries*

[4] *a journey to a sacred place; see glossary*

[5] *pilgrims*

[6] *shores*

[7] *various*

[8] *countryside's*

[9] *go*

[10] *Thomas à Becket, who was martyred at Canterbury; see glossary*

[11] *an area south of London bridge; in Chaucer's time, it had many inns and taverns.*

[12] *the inn where the pilgrims are staying*

Some nine and twenty in a company
25 Of sundry persons who had chanced to fall
In fellowship, and pilgrims were they all
That toward Canterbury town would ride.
The rooms and stables spacious were and wide,
And well we there were eased, and of the best.
30 And briefly, when the sun had gone to rest,
So had I spoken with them, every one,
That I was of their fellowship anon,
And made agreement that we'd early rise
To take our way, as to you I'll devise.[13]
35 But nonetheless, whilst I have time and space,
Before yet farther in this tale I pace,
It seems to me accordant with reason
To inform you of the state of every one
Of all of these, as it appeared to me,
40 And who they were, and what was their degree,
And also what array[14] they all were in;
And with a knight thus will I first begin.

THE KNIGHT

A knight there was, and he a worthy man,
Who, from the moment that he first began
To ride about the world, loved chivalry,[15]
Truth, honour, freedom and all courtesy.
5 Full worthy was he in his liege-lord's war,
And therein had he ridden (none more far)
As well in Christendom as heathenesse,[16]
And honored everywhere for worthiness.
At Alexandria,[17] he, when it was won;
10 Full oft the table's roster he'd begun[18]
Above all nations' knights in Prussia.
In Latvia raided he, and Russia,
No christened man so oft of his degree.[19]
In far Granada at the siege was he
15 Of Algeciras,[20] and in Belmarie.[21]
At Ayas was he and at Satalye[22]
When they were won; and on the Middle Sea[23]
At many a noble meeting chanced to be.

[13]*recount*

[14]*dress*

[15]*the code of behavior for knights*

[16]*heathen lands*

[17]*the site of a Crusade; see glossary*

[18]*He often sat at the head of the table.*

[19]*Few men participated in as many battles as he did.*

[20]*a city in Southern Spain*

[21]*a city in Morocco*

[22]*two cities in Turkey*

[23]*Mediterranean Sea*

And he'd fought for our faith at Tramissene[24]
Of mortal battles he had fought fifteen,
20 Three times in lists,[25] and each time slain his foe.
This self-same knight had been also
At one time with the lord of Palatye[26]
Against another heathen in Turkey:
And always won he sovereign fame for prize.
25 Though so illustrious, he was very wise
And bore himself as meekly as a maid.
He never yet had any vileness said,
In all his life, to whatsoever wight.[27]
He was a truly perfect, gentle knight.
30 But now, to tell you all of his array,
His steeds were good, but yet he was not gay.
Of simple fustian[28] wore he a jupon[29]
Sadly discoloured by his habergeon;[30]
For he had lately come from his voyage
35 And now was going on this pilgrimage.

THE SQUIRE[31]

With him there was his son, a youthful squire,
A lover and a lusty bachelor,
With locks well curled, as if they'd laid in press.
Some twenty years of age he was, I guess.
5 In stature he was of an average length,
Wondrously active, aye, and great of strength.
He'd ridden sometime with the cavalry
In Flanders, in Artois, and Picardy,[32]
And borne him well within that little space
10 In hope to win thereby his lady's grace.
Embroidered was he, like a meadow bed
All full of freshest flowers, white and red.
Singing he was, or fluting, all the day;
He was as fresh as is the month of May.
15 Short was his gown, with sleeves both long and wide.[33]
Well could he sit on horse, and fairly ride.
He could make songs and words thereto indite,
Joust, and dance too, as well as sketch and write.[34]
So hot he loved that, while night told her tale,

[24] *a city in modern-day Algeria*

[25] *duels*

[26] *a city in Turkey*

[27] *man*

[28] *coarse cloth*

[29] *sleeveless jacket*

[30] *chainmail vest*

[31] *a gentleman ranked below a knight*

[32] *sites in France and the Netherlands where English knights fought*

[33] *the fashion of the day*

[34] *Literacy was not widespread at this time, so this is a mark of the squire's class.*

20 He slept no more than does a nightingale.
    Courteous he, and humble, willing and able,
    And carved before his father at the table.

THE YEOMAN[35]

[35]a high-ranking servant

    A yeoman had he, nor more servants, no,
    At that time, for he chose to travel so;
    And he was clad in coat and hood of green.
    A sheaf of peacock arrows bright and keen
 5 Under his belt he bore right carefully
    (Well could he keep his tackle yeomanly:
    His arrows had no draggled feathers low),
    And in his hand he bore a mighty bow.
    A cropped head had he and a sun-browned face.
10 Of woodcraft knew he all the useful ways.
    Upon his arm he bore a bracer[36] gay,
    And at one side a sword and buckler,[37] yea,
    And at the other side a dagger bright,
    Well sheathed and sharp as spear point in the light;
15 On breast a Christopher of silver sheen.[38]
    He bore a horn in baldric[39] all of green;
    A forester he truly was, I guess.

[36]arm guard

[37]shield

[38]Christopher was the patron saint of travelers.

[39]sash

THE PRIORESS[40]

[40]the supervisor of an abbey

    There was also a nun, a prioress,
    Who, in her smiling, modest was and coy;
    Her greatest oath was but "By Saint Eloy!"[41]
    And she was known as Madam Eglantine.[42]
 5 Full well she sang the services divine
    Intoning through her nose, becomingly;
    And fair she spoke her French,[43] and fluently,
    After the school of Stratford-at-the-Bow,[44]
    For French of Paris was not hers to know.
10 At table she had been well taught withal,
    And never from her lips let morsels fall,
    Nor dipped her fingers deep in sauce, but ate

[41]or St. Eligius; the patron saint of goldsmiths

[42]Her name means "honeysuckle."

[43]usually spoken by the upper classes

[44]a city outside of London

With so much care the food upon her plate
That never driblet fell upon her breast.[45]
15 In courtesy she had delight and zest.
Her upper lip was always wiped so clean
That in her cup was no iota seen
Of grease, when she had drunk her draught of wine.
Becomingly, she reached for meat to dine.
20 And certainly she was of great disport[46]
And full pleasant, and amiable of port[47]
And went to many pains to put on cheer
Of court, and very dignified appear,
And to be thought worthy of reverence.
25 But, to say something of her moral sense,
She was so charitable and piteous
That she would weep if she but saw a mouse
Caught in a trap, though it were dead or bled.
She had some little dogs, too, that she fed
30 On roasted flesh, or milk and fine white bread.[48]
But sore she'd weep if one of them were dead,
Or if men smote it with a rod to smart:
For pity ruled her, and her tender heart.
Full properly her wimple[49] pleated was.
35 Her nose was straight, her eyes as grey as glass,
Her mouth full small, and also soft and red;
But certainly she had a fair forehead;
It was almost a full span broad,[50] I own,
For, truth to tell, she was not undergrown.
40 Full stylish was her cloak, I was aware.
Of coral small about her arm she'd bear
A string of beads,[51] gauded[52] all round with green;
And from there hung a brooch of golden sheen
On which there was first written a crowned "A,"
45 And under, Amor Vincit Omnia.[53]
Another little nun with her had she,
Who was her chaplain;[54] and of priests, she had three.

[45]*Notice the nun's dainty manners; where is her attention focused?*

[46]*Well-bred ladies were supposed to be cheerful at social events.*

[47]*behavior*

[48]*This kind of bread was very expensive.*

[49]*nun's head covering*

[50]*Broad foreheads were highly fashionable.*

[51]*rosary beads*

[52]*interspersed*

[53]*"Love Conquers All"*

[54]*a Prioress's secretary*

[55]clergymen who swore to withdraw from "worldly" affairs and live in a monastery; see glossary

[56]a monk who travels the countryside

[57]hunting

[58]a disciple of St. Benedict

[59]the founder of the Benedictine Rule, a guide to daily living for monks

[60]toil

[61]St. Augustine, one of the Four Fathers of the Catholic Church

THE MONK[55]

A monk there was, one made for mastery,
An outrider,[56] who loved his venery;[57]
A manly man, to be an abbot able.
Full many a blooded horse had he in stable:
5 And when he rode men might his bridle hear
A-jingling in the whistling wind as clear,
Aye, and as loud as does the chapel bell
Where this brave monk was master of the cell.
The rule of Maurus[58] or Saint Benedict,[59]
10 By reason it was old and somewhat strict,
This said monk let such old things slowly pace
And followed new-world manners in their place.
He cared not for that text a clean-plucked hen
Which holds that hunters are not holy men
15 Nor that a monk, when he is cloisterless,
Is like unto a fish that's waterless;
That is to say, a monk out of his cloister.
But this same text he held not worth an oyster;
And I said his opinion was right good.
20 What? Should he study as a madman would
Upon a book in cloister cell? Or yet
Go labour with his hands and swink[60] and sweat,
As Austin[61] bids? How shall the world be served?
Let Austin have his swink to him reserved!
25 Therefore he was a rider day and night;
Greyhounds he had, as swift as fowl in flight.
Since riding and the hunting of the hare
Were all his love, for no cost would he spare.
I saw his sleeves were lined around the hand
30 With fur of grey, the finest in the land;
Also, to fasten hood beneath his chin,
He had of good wrought gold a curious pin:
A love-knot in the larger end there was.
His head was bald and shone like any glass
35 And smooth as one anointed was his face.
Fat was this lord, he stood in goodly case.
His bulging eyes he rolled about, and hot
They gleamed, and red, like fire beneath a pot;

His boots were soft; his horse of great estate.
40 Now certainly he was a fine prelate:[62]
He was not pale as some poor wasted ghost.
A fat swan loved he best of any roast.
His palfrey[63] was as brown as is a berry.

THE FRIAR[64]

A friar there was, a wanton and a merry,
A limiter,[65] a very worthy man.
In all the Orders Four[66] is none that can
Equal his friendliness and fair language.
5 He had arranged full many a marriage
Of young women, and this at his own cost.
Unto his order he was a noble post.
Well liked by all and intimate was he
With franklins[67] everywhere in his country,
10 And with the worthy women of the town.
For very sweetly did he hear confession
And pleasant also was his absolution.[68]
He was an easy man to give penance[69]
When knowing he should gain a good pittance;[70]
15 For to a begging friar, money given
Is sign that any man has been well shriven.[71]
For if one gave (he dared to boast of this),
He took the man's repentance not amiss.
For many a man there is so hard of heart
20 He cannot weep however pains may smart.
Therefore, instead of weeping and of prayer,
Men ought to give some silver to the poor freres.
His tippet[72] was stuck always full of knives
And pins, to give to young and pleasing wives.
25 And certainly he kept a merry note:
Well could he sing and play upon the rote.[73]
At balladry he bore the prize away.
His throat was white as lily of the May;
Yet strong he was as any champion.
30 In towns he knew the taverns, every one,
And every host and gay barmaid also

[62]*priest*

[63]*horse*

[64]*a clergyman who, unlike a monk, was supposed to tend to the affairs of the outside world; friars supported themselves by begging.*

[65]*a friar licensed to beg in certain districts*

[66]*Augustinian, Dominican, Carmelite, Franciscan*

[67]*landowners*

[68]*implying that the friar exchanged forgiveness for sexual favors*

[69]*forgiveness*

[70]*small fee*

[71]*having made confession*

[72]*hood*

[73]*fiddle*

Better than beggars and lepers did he know.
For unto no such solid man as he
Accorded it, as far as he could see,
35 To have sick lepers for acquaintances.
There is no honest advantageousness
In dealing with such poverty-stricken curs;
It's with the rich and with big victuallers.[74]
And so, wherever profit might arise,
40 Courteous he was and humble in men's eyes.
There was no other man so virtuous.
He was the finest beggar of his house;
A certain district being farmed to him,
None of his brethren dared approach its rim;
45 For though a widow had no shoes to show,
So pleasant was his *In principio*,[75]
He always got a farthing[76] ere he went.
He lived by pickings, it is evident.
And he could romp as well as any whelp.[77]
50 On love days[78] could he be of great help.
For he was not like a cloisterer,
With threadbare cope[79] as is the poor scholar,
But he was like a lord or like a pope.
Of double worsted[80] was his semi-cope,
55 That rounded like a bell, as you may guess.
He lisped a little, out of wantonness,
To make his English soft upon his tongue;
And in his harping, after he had sung,
His two eyes twinkled in his head as bright
60 As do the stars within the frosty night.
This worthy limiter was named Hubert.

THE MERCHANT[81]

There was a merchant with forked beard, and girt[82]
In motley[83] gown, and high on horse he sat,
Upon his head a Flemish beaver hat;
His boots were fastened rather elegantly.
5 His spoke his notions out right pompously,
Stressing the times when he had won, not lost.

[74]*food-sellers*

[75]*"In the beginning," the first words of the Old Testament*

[76]*coin*

[77]*puppy*

[78]*days in which legal disputes were settled*

[79]*coat*

[80]*fine-knit*

[81]*England was involved in trade with Flanders (modern-day Holland and Belgium) at this time; the merchant is a typical businessman in this trade.*

[82]*belted*

[83]*multicolored cloth*

He would the sea were held at any cost
Across from Middleburgh to Orwell town.
At money-changing he could make a crown.[84]
10 This worthy man kept all his wits well set;
There was no one could say he was in debt,
So well he governed all his trade affairs
With bargains and with borrowings and with shares.
Indeed, he was a worthy man withal,
15 But, sooth[85] to say, his name I can't recall.

THE CLERK[86]

A clerk from Oxford was with us also,
Who'd turned to getting knowledge, long ago.
As meagre was his horse as is a rake,
Nor he himself too fat, I'll undertake,
5 But he looked hollow and went soberly.
Right threadbare was his overcoat, for he
Had got him yet no churchly benefice,[87]
Nor was so worldly as to gain office.
For he would rather have at his bed's head
10 Some twenty books, all bound in black and red,
Of Aristotle[88] and his philosophy
Than rich robes, fiddle, or gay psaltery.[89]
Yet, and for all he was philosopher,
He had but little gold within his coffer;[90]
15 But all that he might borrow from a friend
On books and learning he would swiftly spend,
And then he'd pray right busily for the souls
Of those who gave him wherewithal for schools.
Of study took he utmost care and heed.
20 Not one word spoke he more than was his need;
And that was said in fullest reverence
And short and quick and full of high good sense.
Pregnant of moral virtue was his speech;
And gladly would he learn and gladly teach.

[84]*coin*

[85]*truth*

[86]*Most literate men were employed by the church; the words* clerk *and* cleric *are related.*

[87]*paying church office*

[88]*an ancient Greek philosopher highly influential in the Middle Ages*

[89]*harp-playing*

[90]*coin depository*

THE LAWYER

[91] *a barrister or lawyer*

[92] *the porch of St. Paul's Cathedral, where people usually consulted lawyers*

[93] *a court in England*

[94] *one who acquires land by dishonest means*

[95] *the right to sell or distribute property*

A sergeant[91] of the law, wary and wise,
Who'd often gone to Paul's walk[92] to advise,
There was also, compact of excellence.
Discreet he was, and of great reverence;
5   At least he seemed so, his words were so wise.
Often he sat as justice in assize,[93]
By patent or commission from the crown;
Because of learning and his high renown,
He took large fees and many robes could own.
10   So great a purchaser[94] was never known.
All was fee simple[95] to him, in effect,
Wherefore his claims could never be suspect.
Nowhere a man so busy of his class,
And yet he seemed much busier than he was.
15   All cases and all judgments could he cite
That from King William's time were apposite.
And he could draw a contract so explicit
Not any man could fault therefrom elicit;
And every statute he'd verbatim quote.

[96] *multi-colored coat*

[97] *stripes*

20   He rode but badly in a medley coat,[96]
Belted in a silken sash, with little bars,[97]
But of his dress no more particulars.

[98] *a landowner*

THE FRANKLIN[98]

[99] *astrological sign*

[100] *bread*

[101] *a philosopher who believed in pursuing sensual pleasures*

[102] *the patron saint of hospitality*

There was a franklin in his company;
White was his beard as is the white daisy.
Of sanguine temperament by every sign,[99]
He loved right well in his morning sop[100] in wine.
5   Delightful living was the goal he'd won,
For he was Epicurus'[101] very son,
That held opinion that a full delight
Was true felicity, perfect and right.
A householder and that a great, was he;
10   Saint Julian[102] he was in his own country.
His bread and ale were always right well done;
A man with better cellars there was none.

Baked meat was never wanting in his house,
Of fish and flesh, and that so plenteous
15 It seemed to snow therein both food and drink
Of every dainty that a man could think.
According to the season of the year
He changed his diet and his means of cheer.
Full many a fattened partridge did he mew,[103]
20 And many a bream[104] and pike in fish-pond too.
Woe to his cook, except the sauces were
Poignant and sharp, and ready all his gear.
His table, waiting in his hall always,
Stood ready covered through the livelong day.
25 At county sessions was he lord and sire,
And often acted as a knight of the shire.[105]
A dagger and a trinket-bag of silk
Hung from his girdle, white as morning milk.
He had been sheriff and been auditor;
30 And nowhere was a worthier vavasor.[106]

THE FIVE GUILDSMEN[107]

A haberdasher[108] and a carpenter,
An arras[109]-maker, dyer, and weaver
Were with us, clothed in similar livery,[110]
All of one sober, great fraternity.
5 Their gear was new and well adorned it was;
Their weapons were not cheaply trimmed with brass,
But all with silver; chastely made and well
Their girdles and their pouches too, I tell.
Each man of them appeared a proper burgess[111]
10 To sit in guildhall on a high dais.[112]
And each of them, for wisdom he could span,
Was fitted to have been an alderman;[113]
For chattels they'd enough, and, too, of rent;
To which their good wives gave a free assent,
15 Or else for certain they had been to blame.
It's good to hear "Madam" before one's name,
And go to church when all the world may see,
Having one's mantle borne right royally.

[103]*coop*

[104]*fish*

[105]*a member of Parliament*

[106]*landholder*

[107]*Craftsmen organized themselves into guilds; see glossary*

[108]*hat-maker*

[109]*curtain*

[110]*uniform*

[111]*citizen of a town*

[112]*platform*

[113]*local official*

THE COOK

A cook they had with them, just for the nones,[114]
To boil the chickens with the marrow-bones,
And flavour tartly and with galingale.[115]
Well could he tell a draught of London ale.
5 And he could roast and seethe and broil and fry,
And make a good thick soup, and bake a pie.
But very ill it was, it seemed to me,
That on his shin a deadly sore[116] had he;
For sweet blanc-mange,[117] he made it with the best.

THE SAILOR

There was a sailor, living far out west;
For aught I know, he was of Dartmouth town.
He sadly rode a hackney,[118] in a gown,
Of thick rough cloth falling to the knee.
5 A dagger hanging on a cord had he
About his neck, and under arm, and down.
The summer's heat had burned his visage brown;
And certainly he was a good fellow.
Full many a draught of wine he'd drawn, I trow,[119]
10 Of Bordeaux vintage, while the trader slept.
Nice conscience was a thing he never kept.
If that he fought and got the upper hand,
By water he sent them home to every land.
But as for craft, to reckon well his tides,
15 His currents and the dangerous watersides,
His harbours, and his moon, his pilotage,
There was none such from Hull[120] to far Carthage.[121]
Hardy, and wise in all things undertaken,
By many a tempest had his beard been shaken.
20 He knew well all the havens, as they were,
From Gottland[122] to the Cape of Finisterre,[123]
And every creek in Brittany[124] and Spain;
His vessel had been christened Madeleine.

[114]occasion

[115]spice

[116][perhaps from the plague]

[117]a white dessert resembling the sore

[118]riding-horse

[119]believe

[120]a port city in northeast England

[121]a city in northern Africa

[122]an island off the coast of Sweden

[123]in northwest Spain

[124]a region of northwest France

THE PHYSICIAN

With us there was a doctor of physic;
10 In all this world was none like him to pick
For talk of medicine and surgery;
For he was grounded in astronomy.[125]
He watched over his patients one and all
By hours[126] of his magic natural.[127]
15 Well could he tell the fortune ascendant
Within he houses for his sick patient.
He knew the cause of every malady,
Were it of hot or cold, of moist or dry,
And where engendered, and of what humour;[128]
20 He was a very good practitioner.
The cause being known, down to the deepest root,
Anon he gave to the sick man his boot.[129]
Ready he was, with his apothecaries,[130]
To send him drugs and all electuaries;[131]
25 By mutual aid much gold they'd always won—
Their friendship was a thing not new begun.
Well read was he in Esculapius
And Deiscorides, and in Rufus,
Hippocrates, and Hali, and Galen,
30 Serapion, Rhazes, and Avicen,
Averrhoës, Gilbert, and Constantine,
Bernard, and Gatisden, and John Damascene.[132]
In diet he was measured as could be,
Including naught of superfluity,
35 But nourishing and easy to digest.
He rarely heeds what Scripture might suggest.
In blue and scarlet he went clad, withal,
Lined with a taffeta and with sendal;[133]
And yet he was right careful of expense;
40 He kept the gold he gained from pestilence.
For gold in physic is a fine cordial,[134]
And therefore loved he gold exceeding all.

[125]*Some ailments and disorders were thought to result from the position of the stars and planets.*

[126]*astronomical measurements of time*

[127]*astrology*

[128]*bodily fluid thought to govern mood*

[129]*cure*

[130]*pharmacists*

[131]*medical mixtures*

[132]*All these people wrote medical treatises.*

[133]*expensive silk*

[134]*tonic*

THE WIFE OF BATH

135*a city in south-west England*

136*Ypres and Ghent were towns in Flanders famous for their cloth.*

There was a housewife come from Bath,135 or near,
Who—sad to say—was deaf in either ear.
At making cloth she had so great a bent
She bettered those of Ypres and even of Ghent.136
5 In all the parish there was no goodwife
Should offering make before her, on my life;
And if one did, indeed, so wroth was she
It put her out of all her charity.
Her kerchiefs were of finest weave and ground;
10 I dare swear that they weighed a full ten pound
Which, of a Sunday, she wore on her head.
Her hose were of the choicest scarlet red,
Close gartered, and her shoes were soft and new.
Bold was her face, and fair, and red of hue.

137*the most important pilgrimage site because it was supposed to be the area in which Jesus preached, was crucified and buried*

15 She'd been respectable throughout her life,
With five churched husbands bringing joy and strife,
Not counting other company in youth;
But thereof there's no need to speak, in truth.
Three times she'd journeyed to Jerusalem;137

138*the seat of the Pope*

139*a pilgrimage site in France*

140*the site of the shrine to Saint James de Compostela*

20 And many a foreign stream she'd had to stem;
At Rome138 she'd been, and she'd been in Boulogne,139
In Spain at Santiago,140 and at Cologne.141
She could tell much of wandering by the way:
Gap-toothed was she, it is no lie to say.
25 Upon an ambler easily she sat,
Well wimpled, aye, and over all a hat
As broad as is a buckler or a targe,142
A rug was tucked around her buttocks large,
And on her feet a pair of spurs quite sharp.

141*a city in Germany that was also an important destination for religious pilgrims*

142*shield*

143*talk*

144*a local priest, whose job was to tend to the spiritual needs of the people in his parish and the surrounding countryside.*

30 In company well could she laugh and carp.143
The remedies of love she knew, perchance,
For of that art she'd learned the old, old dance.

THE PARSON144

There was a good man of religion, too,
A country parson, poor, I warrant you;
But rich he was in holy thought and work.

He was a learned man also, a clerk,
5   Who Christ's own gospel truly sought to preach;
    Devoutly his parishioners would he teach.
    Benign he was and wondrous diligent.
    Patient in adverse times and well content,
    As he was oft times proven; always blithe,
10 He was right loath to curse to get a tithe,[145]
    But rather would he give, in case of doubt,
    Unto those poor parishioners about,
    Part of his income, even of his goods.
    Enough with little, coloured all his moods.
15 Wide was his parish, houses far asunder,
    But never did he fail, for rain or thunder,
    In sickness, or in sin, or any state,
    To visit to the farthest, small and great,
    Going afoot, and in his hand a stave.[146]
20 This fine example to his flock he gave,
    That first he wrought and afterwards he taught;
    Out of the gospel then that text he caught,
    And this figure he added thereunto—
    That, if gold rust, what shall poor iron do?
25 For if the priest be foul, in whom we trust,
    What wonder if a layman yield to lust?
    And shame it is, if priest take thought for keep,
    A shitty shepherd, shepherding clean sheep.
    Well ought a priest example good to give,
30 By his own cleanness, how his flock should live.
    He never let his benefice[147] for hire,
    Leaving his flock to flounder in the mire,
    And ran to London, up to old Saint Paul's[148]
    To get himself a chantry[149] there for souls,
35 Nor in some brotherhood did he withold;
    But dwelt at home and kept so well the fold
    That never wolf could make his plans miscarry;
    He was a shepherd and not mercenary.
    And holy though he was, and virtuous,
40 To sinners he was not impetuous,
    Nor haughty in his speech, nor too divine,
    But in all teaching prudent and benign.
    To lead folk into Heaven but by stress
    Of good example was his busyness.

[145]*the portion of a person's income that was supposed to be set aside for the Church*

[146]*shepherd's staff*

[147]*paid church office*

[148]*the principal cathedral of London*

[149]*an office in which a priest was paid to pray for people; usually a source of easy money*

45 But if some sinful one proved obstinate,
    Be who it might, of high or low estate,
    Him he reproved, and sharply, as I know.
    There is nowhere a better priest, I trow.[150]
    He had no thirst for pomp or reverence,
50 Nor made himself a special, spiced conscience,
    But Christ's own lore, and His apostles' twelve
    He taught, but first he followed it himself.

THE PLOWMAN[151]

    With him there was a plowman, was his brother
    That many a load of dung, and many another
    Had scattered, for a good true toiler, he,
    Living in peace and perfect charity.
5   He loved God most, and that with his whole heart
    At all times, though he played or plied his art
    And next, his neighbour, even as himself.
    He'd thresh and dig, with never thought of pelf,[152]
    For Christ's own sake, for every poor wight
10 All without pay, if it lay in his might.
    He paid his taxes, fully, fairly, well,
    Both by his own toil and by stuff he'd sell.
    In a tabard[153] he rode upon a mare.
    There were also a reeve and miller there;
15 A summoner, maniciple, and pardoner,
    And these, beside myself, made all there were.

THE MILLER[154]

    The miller was a stout churl,[155] be it known,
    Hardy and big of brawn and big of bone;
    Which was well proved, for when he went on lam
    At wrestling, never failed he of the ram.
5   He was a chunky fellow, broad of build;
    He'd heave a door from hinges if he willed,
    Or break it through, by running, with his head.
    His beard, as any sow or fox, was red,

[150]*believe*

[151]*supposed to represent a typical commoner, or member of the "third estate"; see glossary*

[152]*wealth*

[153]*loose shirt*

[154]*Medieval stories sometimes presented millers as dishonest; Chaucer follows suit.*

[155]*rude, coarse man*

And broad it was as if it were a spade.
10 Upon the coping[156] of his nose he had
A wart, and thereon stood a tuft of hairs,
Red as the bristles in an old sow's ears;
His nostrils they were black and very wide.
A sword and buckler bore he by his side.
15 His mouth was like a furnace door for size.
He was a jester and could poetize,
But mostly all of sin and ribaldries.[157]
He could steal corn and full thrice charge his fees;
And yet he had a thumb of gold,[158] begad.
20 A white coat and blue hood he wore, this lad.
A bagpipe he could blow well, be it known,
And with that same he brought us out of town.

THE MANCIPLE[159]

There was a manciple from an inn of court,
To whom all buyers might quite well resort
To learn the art of buying food and drink;
For whether he paid cash or not, I think
5 That he so knew the markets, when to buy,
He never found himself left high and dry.
Now is it not of God a full fair grace
That such a vulgar man has wit to pace
The wisdom of a crowd of learned men?
10 Of masters had he more than three times ten,
Who were in law expert and curious;
Whereof there were a dozen in that house
Fit to be stewards of both rent and land
Of any lord in England who would stand
15 Upon his own and live in manner good,
In honour, debtless (save his head were wood),
Or live as frugally as he might desire;
These men were able to have helped a shire
In any case that ever might befall;
20 And yet this manciple outguessed them all.

[156]*top part*

[157]*obscene stories*

[158]*Millers were said to cheat customers by putting their thumbs on the scale when they weighed grain.*

[159]*someone who purchased supplies for a school or monastery*

THE REEVE[160]

[160]*an official in charge of overseeing a large estate*

[161]*irritable*

[162]*shaved on top, like a monk's*

    The reeve he was a slender, choleric[161] man,
    Who shaved his beard as close as razor can.
    His hair was cut round even with his ears;
    His top was tonsured[162] like a pulpiteer's.
5 Long were his legs, and they were very lean,
    And like a staff, with no calf to be seen.
    Well could he manage granary and bin,
    No auditor could ever on him win.
    He could foretell, by drought and by the rain,
10 The yielding of his seed and of his grain.
    His lord's sheep and his oxen and his dairy,
    His swine and horses, all his stores, his poultry,
    Were wholly in this steward's managing;
    And, by agreement, he'd made reckoning
15 Since his young lord of age was twenty years;
    Yet no man ever found him in arrears.[163]
    There was no agent, hind,[164] or herd[165] who'd cheat
    But he knew well his cunning and deceit;
    They were afraid of him as of the death.
20 His cottage was a good one, on a heath;
    By green trees shaded with this dwelling-place.
    Much better than his lord could he purchase.
    Right rich he was in his own private right,
    Seeing he'd pleased his lord, by day or night,
25 By giving him, or lending, of his goods,
    And so got thanked—but yet got coats and hoods.
    In youth he'd learned a good trade, and had been
    A carpenter, as fine as could be seen.
    This steward sat a horse that well could trot,
30 And was all dapple-grey, and was named Scot.
    A long surcoat[166] of blue did he parade,
    And at his side he bore a rusty blade.
    Of Norfolk[167] was this reeve of whom I tell,
    From near a town that men call Badeswell.
35 Bundled he was like friar from chin to croup,[168]
    And ever he rode hindmost of our troop.

[163]*owing money*

[164]*country laborer*

[165]*shepherd*

[166]*outer coat*

[167]*an area in the East of England*

[168]*the rear of his horse*

THE SUMMONER[169]

A summoner was with us in that place,
Who had a fiery-red, cherubic face,
For eczema he had; his eyes were narrow.
As hot he was, and lecherous, as a sparrow;[170]
5 With black and scabby brows and scanty beard,
He had a face that little children feared.
There was no mercury, sulphur, or litharge,
No borax, ceruse, tartar[171] could discharge,
Nor ointment that could cleanse enough, or bite,
10 To free him of his boils and pimples white,
Nor of the bosses resting on his cheeks.
Well loved he garlic, onions, aye and leeks,
And drinking of strong wine as red as blood.
Then would he talk and shout as madman would.
15 And when a deal of wine he'd poured within,
Then would he utter no word save Latin.[172]
Some phrases had he learned, say two or three,
Which he had garnered out of some decree;
No wonder, for he'd heard it all the day;
20 And all you know right well that even a jay
Can call out "Wat" as well as can the pope.
But when, for aught else, into him you'd grope,
'Twas found he'd spent his whole philosophy;
Just "Questio quid juris"[173] would he cry.
25 He was a noble rascal, and a kind;
A better comrade 'twould be hard to find.
Why, he would suffer, for a quart of wine,
Some good fellow to have his concubine
A twelve-month, and excuse him to the full
30 (Between ourselves, though, he could pluck a gull[174]).
And if he chanced upon a good fellow,
He would instruct him never to have awe,
In such a case, of the archdeacon's curse[175]
Except a man's soul lie within his purse;
35 For in his purse the man should punished be.
"The purse is the archdecon's Hell," said he.
But well I know he lied in what he said;
A curse ought every guilty man to dread
(For curse can kill, as absolution save),

[169]*a man who summoned people to Church court*

[170]*A sparrow was thought to be a highly sexual bird.*

[171]*substances thought to cleanse the skin*

[172]*the language of the Church; the Summoner knows only a few phrases.*

[173]*a phrase used in Church court*

[174]*pull a trick; also, engage in sexual intercourse*

[175]*excommunication*

And 'ware significavit[176] to the grave.
40 In his own power had he, and at ease,
    The boys and girls of all the diocese,
    And knew their secrets, and by counsel led.
    A garland had he set upon his head,
    Large as a tavern's wine-bush on a stake;
45 A buckler had he made of bread they bake.

THE PARDONER[177]

With him there rode a gentle pardoner
Of Rouncival,[178] his friend and his compeer;[179]
Straight from the court of Rome had journeyed he.
Loudly he sang "Come hither, love, to me,"
5 The summoner joining with a burden[180] round;
Was never horn of half so great a sound.
This pardoner had hair as yellow as wax,
But lank it hung as does a strike of flax;
In wisps hung down such locks as he'd on head,
10 And with them he his shoulders overspread;
But thin they dropped, and stringy, one by one.
But as to hood, for sport of it, he'd none,
Though it was packed in wallet all the while.
It seemed to him he went in latest style,
15 Dishevelled, save for cap, his head all bare.
As shiney eyes he had as has a hare,
He had fine veronica sewed to cap.
His wallet lay before him in his lap,
Stuffed full of pardons brought from Rome all hot.
20 A voice he had that bleated like a goat.
No beard had he, nor ever should he have,
For smooth his face as he'd just had a shave;
I think he was a gelding[181] or a mare.
But in his craft, from Berwick unto Ware,[182]
25 Was no such pardoner in any place.
For in his bag he had a pillowcase
The which, he said, was Our True Lady's veil:
He said he had a piece of the very sail
That good Saint Peter[183] had, what time he went
30 Upon the sea, till Jesus changed his bent.

[177]a man who sells
  papal pardons
  for sin

[178]a hospital

[179]companion

[180]bass
  accompaniment

[181]castrated horse

[182]i.e., from one
  side of England to
  another

[183]an apostle
  whom Jesus
  ordered to walk
  upon the water

He had a latten[184] cross set full of stones,
And in a bottle had he some pig's bones.
But with these relics, when he came upon
Some simple parson, then this paragon

35 In that one day more money stood to gain
Than the poor dupe in two months could attain.
And thus, with flattery and suchlike japes,
He made the parson and the rest his apes.
But yet, to tell the whole truth at the last,

40 He was, in church, a fine ecclesiast.
Well could he read a lesson or a story,
But best of all he sang an offertory;
For well he knew that when that song was sung,
Then might he preach, and all with polished tongue,

45 To win some silver, as he right well could;
Therefore he sang so merrily and so loud.
    Now have I told you briefly, in a clause,
The state, the array, the number, and the cause
Of the assembling of this company

50 In Southwark, at this noble hostelry
Known as the Tabard Inn, hard by the Bell.[185]
But now the time is come wherein to tell
How all we bore ourselves that very night
When at the hostelry we did alight.

55 And afterward the story I engage
To tell you of our common pilgrimage.
But first, I pray you, of your courtesy,
You'll not ascribe it to vulgarity
Though I speak plainly of this matter here,

60 Retailing you their words and means of cheer;
Nor though I use their very terms, nor lie.
For this thing do you know as well as I:
When one repeats a tale told by a man,
He must report, as nearly as he can,

65 Every least word, if he remember it,
However rude it be, or how unfit;
Or else he may be telling what's untrue,
Embellishing and fictionalizing too.
He may not spare, although it were his brother;

70 He must as well say one word as another.
Christ spoke right broadly out, in holy writ,

[184]*brass*

[185]*another tavern*

And, you know well, there's nothing low in it.
And Plato says, to those able to read:
"The word should be the cousin to the deed."[186]
75 Also, I pray that you'll forgive it me
If I have not set folk, in their degree
Here in this tale, by rank as they should stand.
My wits are not the best, you'll understand.

[186]"The written word should be as close to what was actually said."

THE HOST

Great cheer our host gave to us, every one,
And to the supper set us all anon;
And served us then with victuals of the best.
Strong was the wine and pleasant to each guest.
5 A seemly man our good host was, withal,
Fit to have been a marshal in some hall;
He was a large man, with protruding eyes,
As fine a burgher[187] as in Cheapside lies;
Bold in his speech, and wise, and right well taught,
10 And as to manhood, lacking there in naught.
Also, he was a very merry man,
And after meat, at playing he began,
Speaking of mirth among some other things,
When all of us had paid our reckonings;
15 And saying thus: "Now masters, verily
You are all welcome here, and heartily:
For by my truth, and telling you no lie,
I have not seen, this year, a company
Here in this inn, fitter for sport than now.
20 Fain would I make you happy, knew I how.
And of a game have I this moment thought
To give you joy, and it shall cost you naught.
   "You go to Canterbury; may God speed
And the blessed martyr soon requite your meed.[188]
25 And well I know, as you go on your way,
You'll tell good tales and shape yourselves to play;
For truly there's no mirth nor comfort, none,
Riding the roads as dumb as is a stone;
And therefore will I furnish you a sport,
30 As I just said, to give you some comfort.

[187]tradesman

[188]reward

And if you like it, all, by one assent,
And will be ruled by me, of my judgment,
And will so do as I'll proceed to say,
Tomorrow, when you ride upon your way,
35 Then, by my father's spirit, who is dead,
If you're not gay, I'll give you up my head.
Hold up your hands, nor more about it speak."
    Our full assenting was not far to seek;
We thought there was no reason to think twice,
40 And granted him his way without advice,
And bade him tell his verdict just and wise,
    "Masters," quoth he, "here now is my advice;
But take it not, I pray you, in disdain;
This is the point, to put it short and plain,
45 That each of you, beguiling the long day,
Shall tell two stories as you wend your way
To Canterbury town; and each of you
On coming home, shall tell another two,
All of adventures he has known befall.
50 And he who plays his part the best of all,
That is to say, who tells upon the road
Tales of best sense, in most amusing mode,
Shall have a supper at the others' cost
Here in this room and sitting by this post,
55 When we come back again from Canterbury.
And now, the more to warrant you'll be merry,
I will myself, and gladly, with you ride
At my own cost, and I will be your guide.
But whosoever shall my rule gainsay
60 Shall pay for all that's bought along the way.
And if you are agreed that it be so,
Tell me at once, or if not, tell me no,
And I will act accordingly. No more."
    This thing was granted, and our oaths we swore,
65 With right glad hearts, and prayed of him, also,
That he would take the office, nor forgo
The place of governor of all of us,
Judging our tales; and by his wisdom thus
Arrange that supper at a certain price,
70 We to be ruled, each one, by his advice
In things both great and small; by one assent,

We stood committed to his government.
And thereupon, the wine was fetched anon;
We drank, and then to rest went every one,
75 And that without a longer tarrying.
    Next morning, when the day began to spring,
Up rose our host, and acting as our cock,
He gathered us together in a flock,
And forth we rode, a jog-trot being the pace,
80 Until we reached Saint Thomas' watering-place.[189]
And there our host pulled horse up to a walk,
And said: "Now, masters, listen while I talk.
You know what you agreed at set of sun.
If even-song and morning-song are one,
85 Let's here decide who first shall tell a tale.
And as I hope to drink more wine and ale,
Whoso proves rebel to my government
Shall pay for all that by the way is spent.
Come now, draw cuts,[190] before we farther win,
90 And he that draws the shortest shall begin.
Sir knight," said he, "my master and my lord,
You shall draw first as you have pledged your word.
Come near," quoth he," my lady prioress:
And you, sir clerk, put by your bashfulness,
95 Nor ponder more; out hands, now, every man!"
    At once to draw a cut each one began,
And, to make short the matter, as it was,
Whether by chance or whatsoever cause,
The truth is, that the cut fell to the knight,
100 At which right happy then was every wight.
Thus that his story first of all he'd tell,
According to the compact, it befell,
As you have heard. Why argue to and fro?
And when this good man saw that it was so,
105 Being a wise man and obedient
To plighted word, given by free assent,
He said: "Since I must then begin the game,
Why, welcome be the cut, and it God's name!
Now let us ride, and hearken what I say."
110   And at that word we rode forth on our way;
And he began to speak, with right good cheer,
His tale anon, as it is written here.

[189]*a stream outside London*

[190]*straws*

The
Knight's
T A L E

ONCE ON A TIME, as old tales tell to us,
There was a duke whose name was Theseus;[1]
Of Athens he was lord and governor,
And in his time was such a conqueror
5   That greater was there not beneath the sun.
Full many a rich country had he won;
What with his wisdom and his chivalry
He gained the realm of Femininity,[2]
That was of old time known as Scythia.[3]
10   There wedded he the queen, Hippolyta,[4]
And brought her home with him to his country.
In glory great and with great pageantry,
And, too, her younger sister, Emily.
And thus, in victory and with melody,
15   Let I this noble duke to Athens ride.
With all his armed host marching at his side.
      And truly, were in not too long to hear,
I would have told you fully how, that year,
Was gained the realm of Femininity
20   By Theseus and by his chivalry;
And all of the great battle that was wrought
Where Amazons and the Athenians fought;
And how was wooed and won Hippolyta,

[1] a legendary Greek king

[2] i.e., the realm of the Amazons, a legendary group of female warriors

[3] a country in Asia Minor

[4] Queen of the Amazons

35

That fair and hardy queen of Scythia;
25 And of the feast was made at their wedding,
And of the tempest at their home-coming;
But all of that I must for now forbear.
I have, God knows, a large field for my share,
And weak the oxen, and the soil is tough.
30 The remnant of the tale is long enough.
I will not hinder any, in my turn;
Let each man tell his tale, until we learn
Which of us all the most deserves to win;
So where I stopped, again I'll now begin.
35   This duke of whom I speak, of great renown,
When he had drawn almost unto the town,
In all well-being and in utmost pride,
He grew aware, casting his eyes aside,
That right upon the road, as suppliants do,
40 A company of ladies, two by two,
Knelt, all in black, before his cavalcade;
But such a clamorous cry of woe they made
That in the whole world living man had heard
No such a lamentation, on my word;
45 Nor would they cease lamenting till at last
They'd clutched his bridle reins and held them fast.
      "What folk are you that at my home-coming
Disturb my triumph with this dolorous thing?"
Cried Theseus. "Do you so much envy
50 My honour that you thus complain and cry?
Or who has wronged you now, or who offended?
Come, tell me whether it may be amended;
And tell me, why are you clothed thus in black?"
      The eldest lady of them answered back,
55 After she'd swooned, with cheek so deathly drear
That it was pitiful to see and hear,
And said: "Lord, to whom Fortune has but given
Victory, and to conquer where you've striven,
Your glory and your honour grieve not us;
60 But we beseech your aid and pity thus.
Have mercy on our woe and our distress.
Some drop of pity, of your gentleness,
Upon us wretched women, oh, let fall!

For see, lord, there is no one of us all
65 That has not been a duchess or a queen;
Now we are captives, as may well be seen:
Thanks be to Fortune and her treacherous wheel,
There's none can rest assured of constant weal.[5]
And truly, lord, expecting your return,
70 In Pity's temple, where the fires yet burn.
We have been waiting through a long fortnight;
Now help us, lord, since it is in your might."

    "I, wretched woman, who am weeping thus,
Was once the wife of King Capaneus,
75 Who died at Thebes, oh, cursed be the day!
And all we that you see in this array,
And make this lamentation to be known,
All we have lost our husbands at that town
During the siege that round about it lay.
80 And now the old Creon, ah welaway!
The lord and governor of Thebes city,
Full of his wrath and all iniquity,
He, in despite and out of tyranny,
To do all shame and hurt to the bodies
85 Of our lord husbands, lying slain awhile,
Has drawn them all together in a pile,
And will not suffer them, nor give consent,
To buried be, or burned, nor will relent,
But sets his dogs to eat them, out of spite."

90   And on that word, at once, without respite,
They all fell prone and cried out piteously:
"Have on us wretched women some mercy,
And let our sorrows sink into your heart!

    This gentle duke down from his horse did start
95 With heart of pity, when he'd heard them speak.
It seemed to him his heart must surely break,
Seeing them there so miserable of the state,
Who had been proud and happy but so late
And in his arms he took them tenderly,
100 Giving them comfort understandingly:
And swore his oath, that as he was true knight,
He would put forth so thoroughly his might
Against the tyrant Creon as to wreak

[5] *good*

105 Vengeance so great that all of Greece should speak
And say how Creon was by Theseus served,
As one that had his death full well deserved.
This sworn and done, he no more there abode;
His banner he displayed and forth he rode
110 Toward Thebes, and all his host marched on beside;
Nor nearer Athens would he walk or ride,
Nor take his ease for even half a day,
But onward, and in camp that night he lay;
And thence he sent Hippolyta the queen
115 And her bright sister Emily, I ween,
Unto the town of Athens, there to dwell
While he went forth. There is no more to tell.

    The image of red Mars, with spear and shield,
So shone upon his banner's snow-white field
120 It made a billowing glitter up and down;
And by the banner borne was his pennon,
On which in beaten gold was worked, complete,
The Minotaur, which he had slain in Crete.
Thus rode this duke, thus rode this conqueror,
125 And in his host of chivalry the flower,
Until he came to Thebes and did alight
Full in the field where he'd intent to fight.
But to be brief in telling of this thing,
With Creon, who was Thebes' dread lord and king,
130 He fought and slew him, manfully, like knight,
In open war, and put his host to flight;
And by assault he took the city then,
Levelling wall and rafter with his men;
And to the ladies he restored again
135 The bones of their poor husbands who were slain,
To do for them the last rites of that day.
But it were far too long a tale to say
The clamour of great grief and sorrowing
Those ladies raised above the bones burning
140 Upon the pyres, and of the great honour
That Theseus, the noble conqueror,
Paid to the ladies when from him they went;
To make the story short is my intent.
When, then, this worthy duke, this Theseus

145 Had slain Creon and won Thebes city thus,
      Still on the field he took that night his rest,
      And dealt with all the land as he thought best.
          In searching through the heap of enemy dead,
      Stripping them of their gear from heel to head,
150 The busy pillagers could pick and choose,
      After the battle, what they best could use;
      And so befell that in a heap they found,
      Pierced through with many a grievous, bloody wound,
      Two young knights lying together, side by side,
155 Bearing one crest, wrought richly, of their pride,
      And of those two Arcita was the one,
      The other knight was known as Palamon.
      Not fully quick, nor fully dead they were,
      But by their coats of arms and by their gear
160 The heralds readily could tell, withal,
      That they were of the Theban blood royal,
      And that they had been of two sisters born.
      Out of the heap the spoilers had them torn
      And carried gently over to the tent
165 Of Theseus; who shortly had them sent
      To Athens, there in prison cell to lie
      For ever, without ransom till they die.
      And when this worthy duke had all this done,
      He gathered host and home he rode anon,
170 With laurel crowned again as conqueror;
      There lived he in all joy and all honour
      His term of life; what more need words express?
      And in a tower, in anguish and distress,
      Palamon and Arcita, day and night,
175 Dwelt whence no gold might help them to take flight.
          Thus passed by year by year and day by day,
      Till it fell out, upon a morn in May,
      That Emily, far fairer to be seen
      Than is the lily on its stalk of green,
180 And fresher than is May with flowers new
      (For with the rose's colour strove her hue,
      I know not which was fairer of the two),
      Before the dawn, as was her wont to do,
      She rose and dressed her body for delight;

185 For May will have no sluggards of the night.
That season rouses every gentle heart
And forces it from winter's sleep to start,
Saying: "Arise and show thy reverence."
So Emily remembered to go thence
190 In honour of the May, and so she rose.
Clothed, she was sweeter than any flower that blows;
Her yellow hair was braided in one tress
Behind her back, a full yard long, I guess.
And in the garden, as the sun up-rose,
195 She sauntered back and forth and through each close,
Gathering many a flower, white and red,
To weave a delicate garland for her head;
And like a heavenly angel's was her song.
     The tower tall, which was so thick and strong,
200 And of the castle was the great donjon,
(Wherein the two knights languished in prison,
Of whom I told and shall yet tell, withal),
Was joined, at base, unto the garden wall
Whereunder Emily went dallying.
205 Bright was the sun and clear that morn in spring,
And Palamon, the woeful prisoner,
As was his wont, by leave of his jailer
Was up and pacing round that chamber high,
From which the noble city filled his eye,
210 And, too, the garden full of branches green,
Wherein bright Emily, fair and serene
Went walking and went roving up and down.
This sorrowing prisoner, this Palamon,
Being in the chamber, pacing to and fro,
215 And to himself complaining of his woe,
Cursing his birth, he often cried "Alas!"
And so it was, by chance or other pass,
That through a window, closed by many a bar
Of iron, strong and square as any spar,
220 He cast his eyes upon Emilia,
And thereupon he blenched and cried out "Ah!"
As if he had been smitten to the heart.
     And at that cry Arcita did up-start,
Asking: "My cousin, why what ails you now

225 That you've so deathly pallor on your brow?
      Why did you cry out? Who's offended you?
      For God's love, show some patience, as I do,
      With prison, for it may not different be;
      Fortune has given this adversity.
230 Some evil disposition or aspect
      Of Saturn[6] did our horoscopes affect
      To bring us here, though differently 'twere sworn;
      But so the stars stood when we two were born;
      We must endure it; that, in brief, is plain."

235 This Palamon replied and said again:
      "Cousin, indeed in this opinion now
      Your fancy is but vanity, I trow.
      It's not our prison that caused me to cry.
      But I was wounded lately through the eye
240 Down to my heart, and that my bane will be.
      The beauty of the lady that I see
      There in that garden, pacing to and fro,
      Is cause of all my crying and my woe.
      I know not if she's woman or goddess;
245 But Venus she is verily, I guess.
      And thereupon down on his knees he fell,
      And said: "O Venus,[7] if it be thy will
      To be transfigured in this garden, thus
      Before me, sorrowing wretch, oh now help us

[7]*the goddess of love*

250 Out of this prison to be soon escaped.
      And if it be my destiny is shaped,
      By fate, to die in durance, in bondage,
      Have pity, then upon our lineage
      That has been brought so low by tyranny."
255   And on that word Arcita looked to see
      This lady who went roving to and fro.
      And in that look her beauty struck him so
      That, if poor Palamon is wounded sore,
      Arcita is as deeply hurt, and more.
260 And with a sigh he said then, piteously:
      "The virgin beauty slays me suddenly
      Of her that wanders yonder in that place;
      And save I have her pity and her grace,
      That I at least may see her day by day,

265 I am but dead; there is no more to say."
    This Palamon, when these words he had heard,
Pitilessly he watched him, and answered:
"Do you say this in earnest or in play?"
    "Nay," quoth Arcita, "earnest, now, I say!
270 God help me, I am in no mood for play!
    Palamon knit his brows and stood at bay.
"It will not prove," he said, "to your honour
After so long a time to turn traitor
To me, who am your cousin and your brother.
275 Sworn as we are, and each unto the other,
That never, though for death in any pain,
Never, indeed, till death shall part us twain,
Either of us in love shall hinder other,
No, nor in any thing, O my dear brother;
280 But that, instead you shall so further me
As I shall you. All this we did agree.
Such was your oath and such was mine also.
You dare not now deny it, well I know.
Thus you are of my party, beyond doubt.
285 And now you would all falsely go about
To love my lady, whom I love and serve,
And shall while life my heart's blood may preserve.
Nay, false Arcita, it shall not be so.
I loved her first, and told you all my woe,
290 As to a brother and to one that swore
To further me, as I have said before.
For which you are in duty bound, as knight,
To help me, if the thing lie in your might,
Or else you're false, I say, and downfallen."
295   Then this Arcita proudly spoke again:
"You shall," he said, "be rather false than I;
And that you're so, I tell you utterly;
For paramour[8] I loved her first, you know.
What can you say? You know not, even now,
300 Whether she is a woman or goddess!
Yours is a worship as of holiness,
While mine is love, as of a mortal maid;
Wherefore I told you of it, unafraid,
As to my cousin and my brother sworn.

[8]*earthly love (i.e., object of sexual desire)*

305 Let us assume you loved her first, this morn;
Know you not well the ancient writer's saw
Of 'Who shall give a lover any law?'
Love is a greater law, aye by my pan,
Than man has ever given to earthly man.

310 And therefore statute law and such decrees
Are broken daily and in all degrees.
A man must needs have love, maugre[9] his head.   [9]*despite*
He cannot flee it though he should be dead,
And be she maid, or widow, or a wife.

315 And yet it is not likely that, in life,
You'll stand within her graces; nor shall I;
For you are well aware, aye verily,
That you and I are doomed to prison drear
Perpetually; we gain no ransom here.

320 We strive but as those dogs did for the bone
They fought all day, and yet their gain was none.   [10]*scavenging bird*
Till came a kite[10] while they were still so wroth[11]
And bore the bone away between them both.   [11]*angry*
And therefore, at the king's court, O my brother,

325 It's each man for himself and not for other.
Love if you like; for I love and aye shall;
And certainly, dear brother, that is all.
Here in this prison cell must we remain
And each endure whatever fate ordain."

330   Great was the strife, and long, betwixt the two,
If I had but the time to tell it you,
But to the point. It happened on a day
(To tell the tale as briefly as I may),
A worthy duke men called Pirithous,

335 Who had been friend unto Duke Theseus,
Since the time when they were very small
Was come to visit Athens and to call
His play-fellow, as he was wont to do,
For in this whole world he loved no man so;

340 And Theseus loved him as truly—nay,
So well each loved the other, old books say,
That when one died (it is but truth I tell),
The other went and sought him down in Hell,
But of that tale I have no wish to write.

345 Pirithous loved Arcita, too, that knight,
Having known him in Thebes full many a year;
And finally, at his request and prayer,
And that without a coin of ransom paid,
Duke Theseus released him out of shade,
350 Freely to go wherever he wished, and to
His own devices, as I'll now tell you.
    The compact was, to set it plainly down,
As made between these two of great renown:
That if Arcita, any time, were found,
355 Ever in life, by day or night, on ground
Of any country of this Theseus,
And he were caught, it was concerted thus,
That by the sword he straight should lose his head.
He had no choice, so taking leave he sped.
360 Let him beware, lest he should lose his head!
    How great is Arcita's sorrow now!
How through his heart he feels death's heavy blow;
He weeps, he wails, he cries out piteously;
To slay himself he now waits privately.
365 Said he: "Alas, the day that I was born!
I'm in worse prison, now, and more forlorn;
Now am I doomed eternally to dwell
No more in Purgatory,[12] but in Hell.
Alas, that I have known Pirithous!
370 For else had I remained with Theseus,
Fettered within that cell; but even so
Then had I been in bliss and not in woe.
Only the sight of her that I would serve,
Though I might never her dear grace deserve,
375 Would have sufficed, oh well enough for me!
O my dear cousin Palamon," said he,
"Yours is the victory, and that is sure,
For there, full happily, you may endure.
In prison? Never, but in Paradise!
380 Oh, well has Fortune turned for you the dice,
Who have the sight of her, I the absence.
For possible it is, in her presence,
You being a knight, a worthy and able,
That by some chance, since Fortune's changeable,

[12]according to Catholic theology, the area in which souls needing to be cleansed of sin must wait until they are ready to enter Heaven

385 You may to your desire sometime attain.
But I, that am in exile and in pain,
Stripped of all hope and in so deep despair
That there's no earth nor water, fire nor air,
Nor any creature made of them there is
390 To help or give me comfort, now, in this—
Surely I'll die of sorrow and distress;
Farewell, my life, my love, my joyousness!"
     "Alas! Why is it men so much complain
Of what great God, or Fortune, may ordain,
395 When better is the gift, in any guise,
Than men may often for themselves devise?
One man desires only that great wealth
Which may but cause his death or long ill-health.
One who from prison gladly would be free,
400 At home by his own servants slain might be.
Infinite evils lie therein, 'tis clear;
We know not what it is we pray for here.
We far as he that's drunken as a mouse;
A drunk man knows right well he has a house,
405 But he knows not the way leading thither;
And a drunk man is sure to slip and slither.
And certainly, in this world so fare we;
We furiously pursue felicity,
Yet we go often wrong before we die.
410 This may we all admit and specially I,
Who deemed and held, as I were under spell,
That if I might escape from prison cell,
Then would I find again what joy might heal,
Who now am only exiled from my weal.
415 For since I may not see you, Emily,
I am but dead; there is no remedy."
     And on the other hand, this Palamon,
When that he found Arcita truly gone,
Such lamentation made he, that the tower
420 Resounded of his crying, hour by hour.
The very fetters on his legs were yet
Again with all his bitter salt tears wet.
"Alas!" said he, "Arcita, cousin mine,
With all our strife, God knows, you've won the wine.

425 You're walking, now, in Theban streets, at large,
    And all my woe you may from mind discharge.
    You may, too, since you've wisdom and manhood,
    Assemble all the people of our blood
    And wage a war so sharp on this city
430 That by some fortune, or by some treaty,
    You shall yet have that lady to your wife
    For whom I now must needs lay down my life.
    For surely 'tis in possibility,
    Since you are now at large, from prison free,
435 And are a lord, great is your advantage
    Above my own, who die here in a cage.
    For I must weep and wail, the while I live,
    In all the grief that prison cell may give,
    And now with pain that love gives me, also,
440 Which doubles all my torment and my woe."
        Therewith the fires of jealousy up-start
    Within his breast and burn him to the heart
    So wildly that he seems one, to behold,
    Like seared box tree, or ashes, dead and cold.
445 Then said he: "O you cruel Gods, that sway
    This world in bondage of your laws, for aye,
    And write upon the tablets adamant
    Your counsels and the changeless words you grant,
    What better view of mankind do you hold
450 Than of the sheep that huddle in the fold?
    For man must die like any other beast,
    Or rot in prison, under foul arrest,
    And suffer sickness and misfortune sad,
    And still be oftentimes guiltless, too, by gad!
455   "What management is in this prescience
    That, guiltless, yet torments our innocence?
    And this increases all my pain, as well,
    That man is bound by law, nor may rebel,
    For fear of God, but must repress his will,
460 Whereas a beast may all his lust fulfill.
    And when a beast is dead, he feels no pain;
    But, after death, man yet must weep amain,
    Though in this world he had but care and woe:
    There is no doubt that it is even so.

465 The answer leave I to divines to tell,
But well I know this present world is hell.
Alas! I see a serpent or a thief,
That has brought many a true man unto grief,
Going at large, and where he wills may turn,
470 But I must lie in jail, because Saturn,
and Juno too, both envious and mad,
Have spilled out well-nigh all the blood we had
At Thebes, and desolated her wide walls.
And Venus slays me with the bitter galls
475 Of fear of Arcita, and jealousy."
　　　Now will I leave this Palamon, for he
Is in his prison, where he still must dwell,
And of Arcita will I forthwith tell.
Summer being passed away and nights grown long,
480 Increased now doubly all the anguish strong
Both of the lover and the prisoner.
I know not which one was the woefuller.
For, to be brief about it, Palamon
Is doomed to lie for ever in prison,
485 In chains and fetters till he shall be dead;
And exiled (on the forfeit of his head)
Arcita must remain abroad, nor see,
For evermore, the face of his lady.
　　　You lovers, now I ask you this question:
490 Who has the worse, Arcita or Palamon?
The one may see his lady day by day,
But yet in prison must he dwell for aye.
The other, where he wishes, he may go,
But never see his lady more, ah no.
495 Now answer as you wish, all you that can,
For I will speak right on as I began.
　　　　　Explicit prima pars.
　　　　　Sequitur pars secunda.[13]
　　　Now when Arcita unto Thebes was come,
500 He lay and languished all day in his home,
Since he his lady nevermore should see,
But telling of his sorrow brief I'll be.
Had never any man so much torture,
No, nor shall have while this world may endure.

[13]*The first part ends here. The second one follows.*

505　Bereft he was of sleep and meat and drink,
　　　That lean he grew and dry as shaft, I think.
　　　His eyes were hollow, awful to behold,
　　　His face was sallow,　pale and ashen-cold,
　　　And solitary kept he and alone,
510　Wailing the whole night long, making his moan.
　　　And if he heard a song or instrument,
　　　Then he would weep ungoverned and lament;
　　　So feeble were his sprits, and so low,
　　　And so changed was he, that no man could know
515　Him by his words or voice, whoever heard.
　　　And in this change, for all the world he fared
　　　As if not troubled by malady of love,
　　　But by that humor dark and grim, whereof
　　　Springs melancholy madness in the brain,
520　And fantasy unbridled holds its reign.
　　　And shortly, all was turned quite upside-down,
　　　Both habits and the temper all had known
　　　Of him, this woeful lover, Sir Arcita.
　　　　　　Why should I all day of his woe indite?
525　When he'd endured all this a year or two,
　　　This cruel torment and this pain and woe,
　　　At Thebes, in his own country, as I said,
　　　Upon a night, while sleeping in his bed,
　　　He dreamed of how the winged God Mercury,[14]
530　Before him stood and bade him happier be.
　　　His sleep-bestowing wand he bore upright;
　　　A hat he wore upon his ringlets bright.
　　　Arrayed this god was (noted at a leap)
　　　As he'd been when to Argus[15] he gave sleep.
535　And thus he spoke: "To Athens shall you wend;
　　　For all your woe is destined there to end."
　　　And on that word Arcita woke and started.
　　　"Now truly, howsoever sore I'm smarted,"
　　　Said he, "to Athens right now will I fare;
540　Nor for the dread of death will I now spare
　　　To see my lady, whom I love and serve;
　　　I will not reck of death, with her, nor swerve."
　　　　　　And with that word he caught a great mirror,
　　　And saw how changed was all his old colour,

[14]the messenger god, who often appears in winged sandals and hat

[15]a hundred-eyed monster once lulled to sleep by Mercury

545   And saw his visage altered from its kind.
      And right away it ran into his mind
      That since his face was now disfigured so,
      By suffering endured (as well we know),
      He might, if he should bear him low in town,
550   Live there in Athens evermore, unknown,
      Seeing his lady well-nigh every day.
      And right anon he altered his array,
      Like a poor labourer in low attire,
      And all alone, save only for a squire,
555   Who knew his secret heart and all his case,
      And who was dressed as poorly as he was,
      To Athens was he gone the nearest way.
      And to the court he went upon a day,
      And offered service to do menial deeds
560   Fetch water, or whatever men should need.
      And to be brief herein, and to be plain,
      He found employment with a chamberlain[16]
      Who was serving in the house of Emily;
      For he was sharp and very soon could see
565   What every servant did who served her there.
      Right well could he hew wood and water bear,
      For he was young and mighty, let me own,
      And big of muscle, aye and big of bone,
      To do what any man asked in a trice.
570   A year or two he was in this service,
      Page of the chamber of Emily the bright;
      He said "Philostrates" would name him right.
      But half so well beloved a man as he
      Was never in that court, of his degree;
575   His gentle nature was so clearly shown,
      That throughout all the court spread his renown.
      They said it were but kindly courtesy
      If Theseus should heighten his degree
      And put him in more honourable service
580   Wherein he might his virtue exercise.
      And thus, anon, his name was so up-sprung,
      Both for his deeds and sayings of his tongue,
      That Theseus had brought him nigh and nigher
      And of the chamber he had made him squire,

[16] *a high-ranking attendant to the king*

585 And given him gold to maintain dignity.
    Besides, men brought him, from his own country,
    From year to year, clandestinely, his rent;
    But honestly and slyly it was spent,
    And no man wondered how he came by it.
590 And three years thus he lived, with much profit,
    And bore him so in peace and so in war
    There was no man that Theseus loved more.
    And in such bliss I leave Arcita now,
    And upon Palamon some words bestow.
595   In darksome, horrible, and strong prison
    These seven years has now sat Palamon,
    Wasted by woe and by his long distress.
    Who has a two-fold heaviness
    But Palamon? whom love yet tortures so
600 That half of his wits he is for woe;
    And joined thereto he is a prisoner,
    Perpetually, not only for a year.
    And who could rhyme in English, properly,
    His martyrdom? Forsooth, it is not I;
605 And therefore I pass lightly on my way.
        It fell out in the seventh year, in May,
    On the third night (as say the books of old
    Which have this story much more fully told),
    Were it by chance or were it destiny
610 (Since, when a thing is destined, it must be),
    That, shortly after midnight, Palamon,
    By helping of a friend, broke from prison,
    And fled the city, fast as he might go;
    For he had given his guard a drink that so
615 Was mixed of spice and honey and certain wine
    And opiates and sleeping powders fine,
    That all that night, although a man might shake
    This jailer, he slept on, nor could awake.
    And thus he flees as fast as ever he may.
620   The night was short and it was nearly day,
    Wherefore he needs must find a place to hide;
    And to a grove that grew hard by, with stride
    Of fearful foot then crept off Palamon.
    In brief, he'd formed his plan, as he went on,

625 That in the grove he would lie fast all day,
       And when night came, then would he take his way
       Toward Thebes, and there find friends, and of them pray
       Their help on Theseus in war's array;
       And briefly either he would lose his life,
630 Or else win Emily to be his wife;
       This is the gist of his intention plain.
           Now I'll return to Arcita again,
       Who little knew how near to him was care
       Till Fortune caught him in her tangling snare.
635 The busy lark, the herald of the day,
       Salutes now in her song the morning grey;
       And fiery Phoebus rises up so bright
       That all the east is laughing with the light,
       And with his streamers dries, among the greves,[17]   [17]*leg-guards*
640 The silver droplets hanging on the leaves.
       And so Arcita, in the court royal
       With Theseus, and his squire principal,
       Is risen, and looks on the merry day.
       And now, to do his reverence to May,
645 Calling to mind the point of his desire,
       He on a courser, leaping high like fire,
       Is ridden to the fields to muse and play,
       Out of the court, a mile or two away;
       And to the grove, whereof I lately told,
650 By accident his way began to hold,
       To make him there the garland that one weaves
       Of woodbine leaves and of green hawthorn leaves.
       And loud he sang within the sunlit sheen:
       "O May, with all thy flowers and all thy green,
655 Welcome be thou, thou fair and freshening May:
       I hope to pluck some garland green today."
       And from his courser, with a lusty heart,
       Into the grove right hastily did start
       And on a path he wandered up and down,
660 Near which, and as it chanced, this Palamon
       Lay in the thicket, where no man might see,
       For sore afraid of finding death was he.
       He knew not that Arcita was so near:
       God knows he would have doubted eye and ear,

665 But it has been a truth these many years
That "Fields have eyes and every wood has ears."
It's well for one to bear himself with poise;
For every day unlooked-for chance annoys.
And little knew Arcita of his friend,
670 Who was so near and heard him to the end,
Where in the bush he sat now, keeping still.

Arcita, having roamed and roved his fill,
And having sung his rondel,[18] lustily,
Into a study fell he, suddenly,
675 As do these lovers in their strange desires,
Now in the trees, now down among the briers,
Now up, now down, like a bucket in a well.
Even as on a Friday, truth to tell,
The sun shines now, and now the rain comes fast,
680 Even so can fickle Venus overcast
The spirits of her people; as her day
Is changeful, so she changes her array.
Seldom is Friday quite like all the week.

Arcite having sung, began to speak,
685 And sat him down, sighing like one forlorn.
"Alas," said he, "the day that I was born!
How long, O Juno,[19] of thy cruelty,
Wilt thou wage bitter war on Thebes city?
Alas! Confounded beyond all reason
690 The blood of Cadmus and of Amphion;[20]
Of royal Cadmus, who was the first man
To build at Thebes, and first the town began,
And first of all the city to be king;
Of his lineage am I, and his offspring,
695 By true descent, and of the stock royal:
And now I'm such a wretched serving thrall,[21]
That he who is my mortal enemy,
I serve him as his squire, and all humbly.
And even more does Juno give me shame,
700 For I dare not acknowledge my own name;
But whereas I was Arcita by right,
Now I'm Philostrates, not worth a mite.
Alas, thou cruel Mars! Alas, Juno!
Thus have your angers all our kin brought low,

[18] a type of poem

[19] Jove's wife and sister; also, the goddess of marriage

[20] important figures in Thebes' history

[21] slave

705 Save only me, and wretched Palamon,
Whom Theseus martyrs yonder in prison.
And above all, to slay me utterly,
Love has his fiery dart so burningly
Struck through my faithful and care-laden heart,
710 My death was patterned ere[22] my swaddling-shirt.   [22]*before*
You slay me with your two eyes, Emily;
You are the cause for which I now must die.
For on the whole of all my other care
I would not set the value of a tare,[23]   [23]*small seed*
715 So I could do one thing to your pleasance!"
And with that word he fell down in a trance
That lasted long; and then he did up-start.
    This Palamon, who thought that through his heart
He felt a cold and sudden sword blade glide,
720 For rage he shook, no longer would he hide.
But after he had heard Arcita's tale,
As he were mad, with face gone deathly pale,
He started up and sprang out of the thicket,
Crying: "Arcita, oh you traitor wicked,
725 Now are you caught, that crave my lady so,
For whom I suffer all this pain and woe,
And are my blood, and know my secrets' store,
As I have often told you heretofore,
And have befooled the great Duke Theseus,
730 And falsely changed your name and station thus:
Either I shall be dead or you shall die.
You shall not love my lady Emily,
But I will love her, and none other, no;
For I am Palamon, your mortal foe.
735 And though I have no weapon in this place,
Being but out of prison by God's grace,
I say again, that either you shall die
Or else forgo your love for Emily.
Choose which you will, for you shall not depart."
740   This Arcita, with scornful, angry heart,
When he knew him and all the tale had heard,
Fierce as a lion, out he pulled a sword
And answered thus: "By God that sits above!
Were it not you are sick and mad for love,

745 And that you have no weapon in this place,
Out of this grove you'd never move a pace,
But meet your death right now, and at my hand.
For I renounce the bond and its demand
Which you assert that I have made with you.
750 What, arrant fool, love's free to choose and do,
And I will have her, spite of all your might!
But in as much as you're a worthy knight
And willing to defend your love, in mail,
Hear now this word: tomorrow I'll not fail

24recognition,
awareness

755 (Without the cognizance24 of any wight)
To come here armed and harnessed as a knight,
And to bring arms for you, too, as you'll see;
And choose the better and leave the worse for me.
And meat and drink this very night I'll bring,
760 Enough for you, and clothes for your bedding.
And if it be that you my lady win
And slay me in this wood that now I'm in,
Then may you have your lady, for all of me."
This Palamon replied: "I do agree."
765 And thus they parted till the morrow morn,
When each had pledged his honour to return.
O Cupido, that knowst not charity!
O despot, that no peer will have with thee!
Truly, 'tis said, that love, like all lordship,
770 Declines, with little thanks, a partnership.
Well learned they that, Arcite and Palamon.
Arcita rode into the town anon,
And on the morrow, ere the dawn, he bore,
Secretly, arms and armour out of store,

25two

775 Enough for each, and proper to maintain
A battle in the field between the twain.25
And in the grove, at time and place they'd set,
Arcita and this Palamon were met.
Each of the two changed colour in the face.
780 For as the hunter in the realm of Thrace
Stands at the clearing with his ready spear,
When hunted is the lion, or the bear,
And through the forest hears him rushing fast,
Breaking the boughs and leaves, and thinks aghast,

785   "Here comes apace my mortal enemy!
     Now, without fail, he must be slain, or I;
     For either I must kill him ere he pass
     Or he will make of me a dead carcass"—
     So fared these men, in altering their hue,
790   So far as each the strength of other knew.
     There was no "good-day" given, no saluting,
     But without word, rehearsal, or such thing,
     Each of them helping, so they armed each other
     As dutifully as he were his own brother;
795   And afterward, with their sharp spears and strong,
     They thrust each at the other wondrous long.
     You might have fancied that this Palamon,
     In battle, was a furious, mad lion,
     And that Arcita was a tiger quite:
800   Like very boars the two began to smite,
     Like boars that froth for anger in the wood.
     Up to the ankles fought they in their blood.
     And leaving them thus fighting fast and fell,
     Forthwith of Theseus I now will tell.
805   Great destiny, minister-general,
     That executes in this world, and for all,
     The needs that God foresaw ere we were born,
     So strong it is that, though the world had sworn
     The contrary of a thing, by yea or nay,
810   Yet sometime it shall fall upon a day,
     Though not again within a thousand years.
     For certainly our wishes and our fears,
     Whether of war or peace, or hate or love,
     All, all are ruled by that Foresight above.
815   This show I now by mighty Theseus,
     Who to go hunting is so desirous
     And specially of the hart of ten, in May,
     That, in his bed, there dawns for him no day
     That he's not clothed and soon prepared to ride
820   With hound and horn and huntsman at his side.
     For in his hunting has he such delight,
     That it is all his joy and appetite
     To be himself the great hart's deadly bane:
     For after Mars, he serves Diana's reign.

825   Clear was the day, as I have told ere this,
When Theseus, compact of joy and bliss,
With his Hippolyta, the lovely queen,
And fair Emilia, clothed all in green,
A-hunting they went riding royally.
830 And to the grove of trees that grew hard by,
In which there was a hart,[26] as men had told,
Duke Theseus the shortest way did hold.
And to the glade he rode on, straight and right,
For there the hart was wont to go in flight,
835 And over a brook, and so forth on his way.
This duke would have a course at him today,
With such hounds as it pleased him to command.
      And when this duke was come upon that land,
Under the slanting sun he looked, anon,
840 And there saw Arcita and Palamon
Who furiously fought, as two boars do;
The bright swords went in circles to and fro
So terribly, that even their least stroke
Seemed powerful enough to fell an oak;
845 But who the two were, nothing did he note.
This duke his courser with the sharp spurs smote
And in one bound he was between the two
And lugged his great sword out, and cried out: "Ho!
No more, I say, on pain of losing head!
850 By mighty Mars, that one shall soon be dead
Who smites another stroke that I may see!
But tell me now what manner of men ye be
That are so hardy as to fight out here
Without a judge or other officer,
855 As if you rode in lists[27] right royally?"
      This Palamon replied, then, hastily,
Saying: "O Sire, what need for more ado?
We have deserved our death at hands of you.
Two woeful wretches are we, two captives
860 That are encumbered by our own sad lives;
And as you are a righteous lord and judge
Give us not either mercy or refuge
But slay me first, for sacred charity,
But slay my fellow here, as well, with me.

[26] deer

[27] jousting matches

865 Or slay him first; for though you've just learned it,
     This is your foe, the prisoner Arcit
     That from the land was banished, on his head.
     And for the which he merits to be dead.
     For this is he who came unto your gate,
870 And said that he was known as Philostrate
     Thus has he fooled you well this many a year,
     And you have made him your chief squire, I hear:
     And this is he that loves fair Emily.
     For since the day is come when I must die,
875 I make confession plainly and say on,
     That I am that same woeful Palamon
     Who has your prison broken, viciously.
     I am your mortal foe, and it is I
     Who love so hotly Emily the bright
880 That I'll die gladly here within her sight.
     Therefore do I ask death as penalty;
     But slay my fellow with the same mercy,
     For both of us deserve but to be slain."
        This worthy duke presently spoke again,
885 Saying: "This judgment needs but a short session:
     Your own mouth, aye, and by your own confession,
     Has doomed and damned you, as I shall record.
     There is no need for torture, on my word.
     But you shall die, by mighty Mars the red!"
890 But then the queen, whose heart for pity bled,
     Began to weep, and so did Emily
     And all the ladies in the company.
     Great pity must it be, so thought they all,
     That ever such misfortune should befall:
895 For these were gentlemen, of great estate,
     And for no thing, save love, was their debate.
     They saw their bloody wounds, so sore and wide,
     And all cried out—greater and less, they cried
     "Have mercy, lord, upon us women all!"
900 And down upon their bare knees did they fall,
     and would have kissed his feet there where he stood,
     Till at the last assuaged was his high mood;
     For soon will pity flow through gentle heart.
     And though he first for ire did shake and start,

905 He soon considered, to state the case in brief,
    What cause they had for fighting, what for grief;
    And though his anger still their guilt accused,
    Yet in his reason he held them both excused;
    In such wise: he thought well that every man
910 Will help himself in love, if he but can,
    And will himself deliver from prison;
    And, too, at heart he had compassion on
    Those women, for they cried and wept as one;
    And in his gentle heart he thought anon,
915 And softly to himself he said then: "Fie
    Upon a lord that will have no mercy,
    But acts the lion, both in word and deed,
    To those repentant and in fear and need,
    As well as to the proud and pitiless man
920 That still would do the thing he began!
    That lord must surely in discretion lack
    Who, in such case, can no distinction make,
    But weighs both proud and humble in one scale."
       And shortly, when his ire was thus grown pale,
925 He looked up to the sky, with eyes alight,
    And spoke these words, as he would promise plight:

28 *goodness*

    "The god of love, ah benedicite![28]
    How mighty and how great a lord is he!
    Against his might may stand no obstacles,
930 A true god is he by his miracles;
    For he can manage, in his own sweet wise,
    The heart of anyone as he devise.
    Lo, here, Arcita and this Palamon,
    That were delivered out of my prison,
935 And might have lived in Thebes right royally,
    Knowing me for their mortal enemy,
    And also that their lives lay in my hand;
    And yet their love has willed them to this land,
    Against all sense, and brought them here to die!
940 Look you now, is not that a folly high?
    Who can be called a fool, except he love?
    And see, for sake of God who sits above,
    See how they bleed! Are they not well arrayed?
    Thus has their lord, the god of love, repaid

945 Their wages and their fees for their service!
And yet they are supposed to be full wise
Who serve love well, whatever may befall!
But this is yet the best jest of them all,
That she for whom they have this jollity
950 Can thank them for it quite as much as me;
She knows no more of all this fervent fare,
By God! than knows a cuckoo or a hare.
But all must be essayed, both hot and cold,
A man must play the fool, when young or old;
955 I know it of myself from years long gone:
For of love's servants I've been numbered one.
And therefore, since I know well all love's pain,
And know how sorely it can man constrain,
As one that has been taken in the net,
960 I will forgive your trespass, and forget,
At instance of my sweet queen, kneeling here,
Aye, and of Emily, my sister dear.
And you shall presently consent to swear
That nevermore will you my power dare,
965 Nor wage war on me, either night or day,
But will be friends to me in all you may;
I do forgive this trespass, full and fair."
  And then they swore what he demanded there,
And, of his might, they of his mercy prayed,
970 And he extended grace, and thus he said:
"To speak for royalty's inheritress,
Although she be a queen or a princess,
Each of you both is worthy, I confess,
When comes the time to wed: but nonetheless
975 I speak now of my sister Emily,
The cause of all this strife and jealousy—
You know yourselves she may not marry two
At once, although you fight or what you do:
One of you, then, and be he loath or lief,[29]
980 Must pipe his sorrows in an ivy leaf.
That is to say, she cannot have you both,
However jealous one may be, or wroth.
Therefore I put you both in this decree,
That each of you shall learn his destiny

[29]*eager*

985 As it is cast, and hear, now, in what wise
      The word of fate shall speak through my device."
        "My will is this, to draw conclusion flat,
      Without reply, or plea, or caveat[30]
      (In any case, accept it for the best),
990 That each of you shall follow his own quest,
      Free of all ransom or of fear from me;
      And this day, fifty weeks hence, both shall be
      Here once again, each with a hundred knights,
      Armed for the lists, who stoutly for your rights
995 Will ready be to battle, to maintain
      Your claim to love. I promise you, again,
      Upon my word, and as l am a knight,
      That whichsoever of you wins the fight,
      That is to say, whichever of you two
1000 May with his hundred, whom I spoke of, do
      His foe to death, or out of boundary drive,
      Then he shall have Emilia to wive
      To whom Fortuna gives so fair a grace.
      The lists shall be erected in this place.
1005 And God so truly on my soul have ruth
      As I shall prove an honest judge, in truth.
      You shall no other judgment in me waken
      Than that the one shall die or else be taken.
      And if you think the sentence is well said,
1010 Speak your opinion, that you're well repaid.
      This is the end, and I conclude hereon."
      Who looks up lightly now but Palamon?
      Who leaps for you but Arcita the knight?
      And who could tell, or who could ever write
1015 The jubilation made within that place
      Where Theseus has shown so fair a grace?
      But down on knee went each one for delight
      And thanked him there with all his heart and might,
      And specially those Thebans did their part.
1020 And thus, with high hopes, being blithe of heart,
      They took their leave; and homeward did they ride
      To Thebes that sits within her old walls wide.
              Explicit secunda pars.
              Sequitur pars tercia.[31]

1025 I think that men would deem it negligence
    If I forgot to tell of the expense
    Of Theseus, who went so busily
    To work upon the lists, right royally;
    For such an amphitheatre he made,
1030 Its equal never yet on earth was laid.
    The circuit, rising, hemmed a mile about,
    Walled all of stone and moated deep without.
    Round was the shape as compass ever traces,
    And built in tiers, the height of sixty paces,
1035 That those who sat in one tier, or degree,
    Should hinder not the folk behind to see.
    Eastward there stood a gate of marble white.
    And westward such another, opposite.
    In brief, no place on earth, and so sublime,
1040 Was ever made in so small space of time;
    For in the land there was no craftsman quick
    At plane geometry or arithmetic,
    No painter and no sculptor of hard stone,
    But Theseus pressed meat and wage upon
1045 To build that amphitheatre and devise.
    And to observe all rites and sacrifice,
    Over the eastern gate, and high above,
    For worship of Queen Venus, god of love,
    He built an altar and an oratory;
1050 And westward, being mindful of the glory
    Of Mars, he straightway built such another
    As cost a deal of gold and many a bother.
    And northward, in a turret on the wall,
    Of alabaster white and red coral,
1055 An oratory splendid as could be,
    In honour of Diana's chastity,
    Duke Theseus wrought out in noble wise.
    But yet have forgot to advertise
    The noble carvings and the portraitures,
1060 The shapes, the countenances, the figures
    That all were in these oratories three.
    First, in the temple of Venus, one might see,
    Wrought on the wall, and piteous to behold,
    The broken slumbers and the sighing cold,

1065 The sacred tears and the lamenting dire,
      The fiery throbbing of the strong desire,
      That all love's servants in this life endure;
      The vows that all their promises assure;
      Pleasure and hope, desire, foolhardiness,
1070 Beauty, youth, bawdiness, and riches, yes,
      Charms, and all force, and lies, and flattery,
      Expense, and labour; aye, and Jealousy
      That wore of marigolds a great garland
      And had a cuckoo sitting on her hand;
1075 Carols and instruments and feasts and dances,
      Lust and array, and all the circumstances
      Of love that I may reckon or ever shall,
      In order they were painted on the wall,
      Aye, and more, too, than I have ever known.
1080 For truly, all the Mount of Citheron,[32]
      Where Venus has her chief and favoured dwelling,
      Was painted on that wall, beyond my telling,
      With all the gardens in their loveliness.
      Nor was forgot the gate-guard Idleness,
1085 Nor fair Narcissus[33] of the years long gone,
      Nor yet the folly of King Solomon,[34]
      No, nor the giant strength of Hercules,
      Nor Circe's and Medea's sorceries,[35]
      Nor Turnus[36] with his hardy, fierce courage,
1090 Nor the rich Croesus,[37] captive in his age.
      Thus may be seen that wisdom, nor largess,
      Beauty, nor skill, nor strength, nor hardiness,
      May with Queen Venus share authority;
      For as she wills, so must the whole world be.
1095 Lo, all these folk were so caught in her snare
      They cried aloud in sorrow and in care.
      Here let suffice examples one or two,
      Though I might give a thousand more to you.
      The form of Venus, glorious as could be,
1100 Was naked, floating on the open sea,
      And from the navel down all covered was
      With green waves, bright as ever any glass.
      A citole[38] in her small right hand had she,
      And on her head, and beautiful to see,

[32]Cytherea, an island near where Aphrodite was born

[33]the person for whom Echo died

[34]the biblical king who had many wives

[35]famous women who enchanted men to fall in love with them

[36]the man who fought Aeneas (and lost his life) out of his love for Lavinia

[37]a king of Lydia

[38]a cittern, a stringed instrument that resembles a guitar

1105 A garland of red roses, sweet smelling,
       Above her swirled her white doves, fluttering.
       Before her stood her one son, Cupido,
       Whose two white wings upon his shoulders grow;
       And blind he was, as it is often seen;
1110 A bow he bore, and arrows bright and keen.
       Why should I not as well, now, tell you all
       The portraiture that was upon the wall
       Within the fane of mighty Mars the red?
       In length and breadth the whole wall was painted
1115 Like the interior of that grisly place,
       The mighty temple of great Mars in Thrace,
       In that same cold and frosty region where
       Mars to his supreme mansion may repair.
       First, on the wall was limned a vast forest
1120 Wherein there dwelt no man nor any beast,
       With knotted, gnarled, and leafless trees, so old
       The sharpened stumps were dreadful to behold;
       Through which there ran a rumbling, even now,
       As if a storm were breaking every bough;
1125 And down a hill, beneath a sharp descent,
       The temple stood of Mars armipotent,[39]
       Wrought all of burnished steel, whereof the gate
       Was grim like death to see, and long, and strait.
       And therefrom raged a wind that seemed to shake
1130 The very ground, and made the great doors quake.
       The northern light in at those same doors shone,
       For window in that massive wall was none
       Through which a man might any light discern.
       The doors were all of adamant eterne,
1135 Rivetted on both sides, and all along,
       With toughest iron; and to make it strong,
       Each pillar that sustained this temple grim
       Was thick as tun, of iron bright and trim.
       There saw I first the dark imagining
1140 Of felony, and all the compassing;
       And cruel anger, red as burning coal;
       Pickpurses, and the dread that eats the soul;
       The smiling villain, hiding knife in cloak;
       The farm barns burning, and the thick black smoke;

[39]*well-armed*

1145 The treachery of murder done in bed;
      The open battle, with the wounds that bled;
      Contest, with bloody knife and sharp menace;
      And loud with creaking was that dismal place.
      The slayer of himself, too, saw I there,
1150 His very heart's blood matted in his hair;
      The nail that's driven in the skull by night;
      The cold plague-corpse, with gaping mouth upright
      In middle of the temple sat Mischance,
      With gloomy, grimly woeful countenance.
1155 And saw I Madness laughing in his rage;
      Armed risings, and outcries, and fierce outrage;
      The carrion in the bush, with throat wide carved;
      A thousand slain, nor one by plague, nor starved.
      The tyrant, with the spoils of violent theft;
1160 The town destroyed, in ruins, nothing left.
      And saw I burnt the ships that dance by phares,[40]
      The hunter strangled by the fierce wild bears;
      The sow chewing the child right in the cradle;
      The cook well scalded, spite of his long ladle.
1165 Nothing was lacking of Mars' evil part:
      The carter over-driven by his cart,
      Under a wheel he lay low in the dust.
      There were likewise in Mars' house, as needs must,
      The surgeon, and the butcher, and the smith
1170 Who forges sharp swords and great ills therewith.
      And over all, depicted in a tower,
      Sat Conquest, high in honour and in power,
      Yet with a sharp sword hanging o'er his head
      But by the tenuous twisting of a thread.
1175 Depicted was the death of Julius,
      Of Nero great, and of Antonius;[41]
      And though at that same time they were unborn,
      There were their deaths depicted to adorn
      The menacing of Mars, in likeness sure;
1180 Things were so shown, in all that portraiture,
      As are fore-shown among the stars above,
      Who shall be slain in war or dead for love.
      Suffice one instance from old plenitude,
      I could not tell them all, even if I would.

[40] near the pharos, the famous lighthouse of Alexandria

[41] Mark Antony

1185 Mars' image stood upon a chariot,
Armed, and so grim that mad he seemed, God wot;
And o'er his head two constellations shone
Of stars that have been named in writings known.
One being Puella, and one Rubeus.[42]

1190 This god of armies was companioned thus:
A wolf there was before him, at his feet,
Red-eyed, and of a dead man he did eat.
A cunning pencil there had limned this story
In reverence of Mars and of his glory.

1195 Now to the temple of Diana chaste,
As briefly as I can, I'll pass in haste,
To lay before you its description well.
In pictures, up and down, the wall could tell
Of hunting and of modest chastity.

1200 There saw I how Callisto[43] fared when she
(Diana being much aggrieved with her)
Was changed from woman into a she-bear,
And after, made into the lone Pole Star;
There was it; I can't tell how such things are.

1205 Her son, too, is a star, as men may see.
There saw I Daphne[44] turned into a tree
(I do not mean Diana, no, but she,
Peneus' daughter, who was called Daphne)
I saw Actaeon[45] made a hart all rude

1210 For punishment of seeing Diana nude;
I saw, too, how his fifty hounds had caught
And him were eating, since they knew him not.
And painted farther on, I saw before
How Atalanta[46] hunted the wild boar;

1215 And Meleager, and many another there,
For which Diana wrought him woe and care.
There saw I many another wondrous tale
From which I will not now draw memory's veil.
This goddess on an antlered hart was set,

1220 With little hounds about her feet, and yet
Beneath her perfect feet there was a moon,
Waxing it was, but it should wane full soon.
In robes of yellowish green her statue was,
She'd bow in hand and arrows in a case.

[42]*famous geomancers, who made prophesies based upon shapes and patterns in the earth*

[43]*the nymph who was transformed by Diana into the Great Bear, Ursa Major*

[44]*the nymph who Apollo fell in love with and who was transformed into a laurel tree to escape his lust*

[45]*the man who accidentally saw Diana bathing and, as a punishment, was transformed into a stag and killed by his hunting dogs*

[46]*the woman for whom Meleager hunted the wild boar*

1225 Her eyes were downcast, looking at the ground.
Where Pluto in his dark realm may be found.
Before her was a woman travailing,
Who was so long in giving birth, poor thing,
That pitifully Lucina[47] did she call,

1230 Praying, "Oh help, for thou may'st best of all!"
Well could he paint, who had this picture wrought,
With many a florin he'd his colours bought,
But now the lists were done, and Theseus,
Who at so great cost had appointed thus

1235 The temples and the circus, as I tell,
When all was done, he liked it wondrous well.
But hold I will from Theseus, and on
To speak of Arcita and Palamon.
      The day of their return is forthcoming,

1240 When each of them a hundred knights must bring
The combat to support, as I have told;
And into Athens, covenant to uphold,
Has each one ridden with his hundred knights,
Well armed for war, at all points, in their mights.

1245 And certainly, 'twas thought by many a man
That never, since the day this world began,
Speaking of good knights hardy of their hands,
Wherever God created seas and lands,
Was, of so few, so noble company.

1250 For every man that loved all chivalry,
And eager was to win surpassing fame,
Had prayed to play a part in that great game;
And all was well with him who chosen was.
For if there came tomorrow such a case,

1255 You know right well that every lusty knight
Who loves the ladies fair and keeps his might,
Be it in England, aye or otherwhere,
Would wish of all things to be present there
To fight for some fair lady. Ben'cite!

1260 'Twould be a pleasant goodly sight to see!
And so it was with those with Palamon.
With him there rode of good knights many a one;
Some would be armoured in a habergeon[48]
And in a breastplate, under light jupon;[49]

[47]*Diana as a fertility goddess*

[48]*a sleeveless coat of chainmail*

[49]*a tunic bearing a coat of arms*

1265 And some wore breast-and back-plates thick and large;
And some would have a Prussian shield, or targe;[50]
Some on their very legs were armoured well,
And carried axe, and some a mace of steel.
There is no new thing, now, that is not old.

[50]*a small, round shield*

1270 And so they all were armed, as I have told,
To his own liking and design, each one.
There might you see, riding with Palamon,
Lycurgus' self, the mighty king of Thrace;
Black was his beard and manly was his face.

1275 The eyeballs in the sockets of his head,
They glowed between a yellow and a red.
And like a griffon[51] glared he round about
From under bushy eyebrows thick and stout.
His limbs were large, his muscles hard and strong.

[51]*a mythical beast with a lion's body and an eagle's head and wings*

1280 His shoulders broad, his arms both big and long,
And, as the fashion was in his country,
High in a chariot of gold stood he,
With four white bulls in traces, to progress.
Instead of coat-of-arms above harness,

1285 With yellow claws preserved and bright as gold,
He wore a bear-skin, black and very old.
His long combed hair was hanging down his back,
As any raven's feather it was black:
A wreath of gold, arm-thick, of heavy weight,

1290 Was on his head, and set with jewels great,
Of rubies fine and perfect diamonds.
About his car there circled huge white hounds,
Twenty or more, as large as any steer,
To hunt the lion or the antlered deer;

1295 And so they followed him, with muzzles bound,
Wearing gold collars with smooth rings and round.
A hundred lords came riding in his rout,
All armed at point, with hearts both stern and stout
With Arcita, in tales men call to mind,

1300 The great Emetreus, a king of Ind,[52]
Upon a bay steed harnessed all in steel,
Covered with cloth of gold, all diapered well,
Came riding like the god of arms, great Mars.
His coat-of-arms was cloth of the Tartars,[53]

[52]*India*

[53]*people from Turkestan, a large area in west and central Asia*

1305 Begemmed with pearls, all white and round and great.
Of beaten gold his saddle, burnished late;
A mantle from his shoulders hung, the thing
Close-set with rubies red, like fire blazing.
His crisp hair all in bright ringlets was run,
1310 Yellow as gold and gleaming as the sun.
His nose was high, his eyes a bright citrine,[54]
His lips were full, his colouring sanguine.[55]
And a few freckles on his face were seen,
None either black or yellow, but the mean;
1315 And like a lion he his glances cast.
Not more than five-and-twenty years he'd past.
His beard was well beginning, now, to spring;
His voice was as a trumpet thundering.
Upon his brows he wore, of laurel green,
1320 A garland, fresh and pleasing to be seen.
Upon his wrist he bore, for his delight,
An eagle tame, as any lily white.
A hundred lords came riding with him there,
All armed, except their heads, in all their gear,
1325 And wealthily appointed in all things.
For, trust me well, that dukes and earls and kings
Were gathered in this noble company
For love and for increase of chivalry.
About this king there ran, on every side,
1330 Many tame lions and leopards in their pride.
And in such wise these mighty lords, in sum,
Were, of a Sunday, to the city come
About the prime, and in the town did light.
This Theseus, this duke, this noble knight,
1335 When he'd conducted them to his city,
And quartered them, according to degree,
He feasted them, and was at so much pains
To give them ease and honour, of his gains,
That men yet hold that never human wit,
1340 Of high or low estate, could better it.
The minstrelsy, the service at the feast,
The great gifts to the highest and the least,
The furnishings of Theseus, rich palace,
Who highest sat or lowest on the dais,

[54] a greenish-yellow color

[55] a reddish color

1345 What ladies fairest were or best dandling,
      Or which of them could dance the best, or sing,
      Or who could speak most feelingly of love,
      Or what hawks sat upon the perch above,
      Or what great hounds were lying on the floor-
1350 Of all these I will make no mention more;
      But tell my tale, for that, I think, is best;
      Now comes the point, and listen if you've zest.

         That Sunday night, ere day began to spring,
      When Palamon the earliest lark heard sing,
1355 Although it lacked two hours of being day
      Yet the lark sang, and Palamon sang a lay.[56]
      With pious heart and with a high courage
      He rose, to go upon a pilgrimage
      Unto the blessed Cytherea's shrine
1360 (I mean Queen Venus,[57] worthy and benign).
      And at her hour he then walked forth apace
      Out to the lists wherein her temple was,
      And down he knelt in manner to revere,
      And from a full heart spoke as you shall hear.
1365   "Fairest of fair, O lady mine, Venus,
      Daughter of Jove and spouse to Vulcanus,[58]
      Thou gladdener of the Mount of Citheron,
      By that great love thou borest to Adon,[59]
      Have pity on my bitter tears that smart
1370 And hear my humble prayer within thy heart.
      Alas! I have no words in which to tell
      The effect of all the torments of my hell;
      My heavy heart its evils can't bewray;
      I'm so confused I can find naught to say.
1375 But mercy, lady bright, that knowest well
      My heart, and seest all the ills I feel,
      Consider and have ruth upon my sore
      As truly as I shall, for evermore,
      Well as I may, thy one true servant be,
1380 And wage a war henceforth on chastity.
      If thou wilt help, thus do I make my vow,
      To boast of knightly skill I care not now,
      Nor do I ask tomorrow's victory,
      Nor any such renown, nor vain glory

[56] *poem set to music*

[57] *the goddess of love*

[58] *the Roman god of fire, blacksmithing, and metalworking*

[59] *a young man who was killed by a wild boar, and was resurrected by Zeus, permitted to live four months of the year with Venus, four months with Proserpine, and*

1385 Of prize of arms, blown before lord and churl,
     But I would have possession of one girl,
     Of Emily, and die in thy service;
     Find thou the manner how, and in what wise.
     For I care not, unless it better be,
1390 Whether I vanquish them or they do me,
     So I may have my lady in my arms.
     For though Mars is the god of war's alarms,
     Thy power is so great in Heaven above,
     That, if it be thy will, I'll have my love.
1395 Thy temple will I worship always so
     That on thine altar, where'er I ride or go,
     I will lay sacrifice and thy fires feed.
     And if thou wilt not so, O lady, cede,
     I pray thee, that tomorrow, with a spear,
1400 Arcita bear me through the heart, just here.
     For I'll care naught, when I have lost my life,
     That Arcita may win her for his wife.
     This the effect and end of all my prayer,
     Give me my love, thou blissful lady fair."

four months free

[60]*prayer*

1405   Now when he'd finished all the orison,[60]
     His sacrifice he made, this Palamon,
     Right piously, with all the circumstance,
     Albeit I tell not now his observance.
     But at the last the form of Venus shook
1410 And gave a sign, and thereupon he took
     This as acceptance of his prayer that day.
     For though the signal came after delay

[61]*prayer, request*

     Yet he knew well that granted was his boon;[61]
     And with glad heart he got him home right soon.

[62]*one of the hours*
between sunrise
and sunset

1415 Three hours unequal[62] after Palamon
     To Venus' temple at the lists had gone,
     Up rose the sun and up rose Emily

[63]*hurry*

     And to Diana's temple did she hie.[63]
     Her maidens led she thither, and with them
1420 They carefully took fire and each emblem,
     And incense, robes, and the remainder all
     Of things for sacrifice ceremonial.
     There was not one thing lacking; I'll but add
     The horns of mead, as was a way they had.

1425 In smoking temple, full of draperies fair,
     This Emily with young heart debonnaire,
     Her body washed in water from a well;
     But how she did the rite I dare not tell,
     Except it be at large, in general;
1430 And yet it was a thing worth hearing all;
     When one's well meaning, there is no transgression;
     But it is best to speak at one's discretion.
     Her bright hair was unbound, but combed withal;
     She wore of green oak leaves a coronal[64]
1435 Upon her lovely head. Then she began
     And did her ceremonies as we're told
     In Statius' *Thebaid* and books of old.[65]
     Two fires upon the altar stone to fan.
     When kindled was the fire, with sober face
1440 Unto Diana spoke she in that place.
          "O thou chaste goddess of the wildwood green,
     By whom all heaven and earth and sea are seen,
     Queen of the realm of Pluto, dark and low,
     Goddess of maidens, that my heart dost know
1455 For all my years, and knowest what I desire,
     Oh, save me from thy vengeance and thine ire
     That on Actaeon fell so cruelly.
     Chaste goddess, well indeed thou knowest that I
     Desire to be a virgin all my life,
1450 Nor ever wish to be man's love or wife.
     I am, thou know'st, yet of thy company,
     A maid, who loves the hunt and venery,[66]
     And to go rambling in the greenwood wild,
     And not to be a wife and be with child.
1455 I do not crave the company of man.
     Now help me, lady, since thou may'st and can,
     By the three beings who are one in thee.
     For Palamon, who bears such love to me,
     And for Arcita, loving me so sore,
1460 This grace I pray thee, not one thing more,
     To send down love and peace between those two,
     And turn their hearts away from me: so do
     That all their furious love and their desire,
     And all their ceaseless torment and their fire

[64]*crown*

[65]*a Roman epic poem telling the tale of Eteocles and Polynices, Oedipus' sons*

[66]*hunting*

1465 Be quenched or turned into another place;
And if it be thou wilt not show this grace,
Or if my destiny be patterned so
That I must needs have one of these same two,
Then send me him that most desires me.
1470 Behold, O goddess of utter chastity,
The bitter tears that down my two cheeks fall.
Since thou art maid and keeper of us all,
My maidenhead[67] keep thou, and still preserve,
And while I live a maid, thee will I serve."
1475   The fires blazed high upon the altar there,
While Emily was saying thus her prayer,
But suddenly she saw a sight most quaint,
For there, before her eyes, one fire went faint,
Then blazed again; and after that, anon,
1480 The other fire was quenched, and so was gone.
And as it died it made a whistling sound,
As do wet branches burning on the ground,
And from the brands' ends there ran out, anon,
What looked like drops of blood, and many a one;
1485 At which so much aghast was Emily
That she was near dazed, and began to cry,
For she knew naught of what it signified;
But only out of terror thus she cried
And wept, till it was pitiful to hear.
1490 But thereupon Diana did appear,
With bow in hand, like any right huntress,
And said "My daughter, leave this heaviness.
Among the high gods it has been affirmed,
And by eternal written word confirmed,
1495 That you shall be the wife of one of those
Who bear for you so many cares and woes;
But unto which of them I may not tell.
Farewell, for I may not here longer dwell.
The fires which do upon my altar burn
1500 Shall show to you, before you home return,
Your fortune with the lovers in this case.
And with that word, the arrows in the chase
Of Diana did clatter loud and ring
And forth she went in mystic vanishing;

[67] chastity

1505 At which this Emily astonished was,
      And said she then: "Ah, what means this, alas!
      I put myself in thy protection here,
      Diana, and at thy disposal dear."
      And home she wended, then, the nearest way.
1510 This is the purport; there's no more to say.
         At the next hour of Mars, and following this,
      Arcita to the temple walked, that is
      Devoted to fierce Mars, to sacrifice
      With all the ceremonies, pagan-wise.[68]
1515 With sobered heart and high devotion, on
      This wise, right thus he said his orison.
      "O mighty god that in the regions hold
      In every realm and every land
      The reins of battle in thy guiding hand,
1520 And givest fortune as thou dost devise,
      Accept of me my pious sacrifice.
      If so it be that my youth may deserve,
      And that my strength be worthy found to serve
      Thy godhead,[69] and be numbered one of thine,
1525 Then pray I thee for ruth on pain that's mine.
      For that same pain and even that hot fire
      Wherein thou once did'st burn with deep desire,
      When thou did'st use the marvelous beauty
      Of fair young wanton Venus, fresh and free,
1530 And had'st her in thine arms and at thy will
      (Howbeit with thee, once, all the chance fell ill,
      And Vulcan caught thee in his net, whenas
      He found thee lying with his wife, alas!)—
      For that same sorrow that was in thy heart,
1535 Have pity, now, upon my pains that smart.
      I'm young, and little skilled, as knowest thou,
      With love more hurt, and much more broken now,
      Than ever living creature was, I'm sure;
      For she who makes me all this woe endure,
1540 Cares not whether I sink or float in this
      And well I know, ere she mercy promise,
      I must with courage win her in the place;
      And well I know, without the help or grace
      Of thee, none of my strength may me avail.

[68]*according to his pagan rituals*

[69]*divine essence*

1545 Then help me, lord, tomorrow not to fail:
        As well as your hot fire now burneth me,
        Ensure that I will then have victory.
        Mine be the toil, and thine the whole glory!
        Thy sovereign temple will I honour most
1550 Of any spot, and toil and count no cost
        To pleasure thee and in thy craft have grace,
        And in thy fane my banner will I place,
        And all the weapons of my company;
        And evermore, until the day I die,
1555 Eternal fire shalt thou before thee find.
        Moreover, to this vow myself I bind:
        My beard, my hair that ripples down so long,
        That never yet has felt the slightest wrong
        Of razor or of shears, to thee I'll give,
1560 And be thy loyal servant while I live.
        Now, lord, have pity on my sorrows sore;
        Give me the victory. I ask no more."
            With ended prayer of Arcita the strong,
        The rings that on the temple door were hung,
1570 And even the doors themselves, rattled so fast
        That this Arcita found himself aghast.
        The fires blazed high upon the altar bright,
        Until the entire temple shone with light;
        And a sweet odour rose up from the ground;
1575 And Arcita whirled then his arm around,
        And yet more incense on the fire he cast,
        And did still further rites; and at the last
        The armour of God Mars began to ring,
        And with that sound there came a murmuring,
1580 Low and uncertain, saying: "Victory!"
        For which he gave Mars honour and glory.
        And thus in joy and hope, which all might dare,
        Arcita to his lodging then did fare,
        Fain[70] of the fight as fowl is of the sun.
1585 But thereupon such quarrelling was begun,
        From this same granting, in the heaven above,
        Twixt lovely Venus, goddess of all love,
        And Mars, the iron god armipotent,[71]
        That Jove[72] toiled hard to make a settlement;

[70]*desiring, eager*

[71]*powerfully armed*

[72]*king of the gods*

1590 Until the sallow Saturn, calm and cold,
Who had so many happenings known of old,
Found from his full experience the art
To satisfy each party and each part.
For true it is, age has great advantage;
1595 Experience and wisdom come with age;
Men may the old outrun, but not outwit.
Thus Saturn, though it scarcely did befit
His nature so to do, devised a plan
To quiet all the strife, and thus began:
1600   "Now my dear daughter Venus," quoth Saturn,
"My course, which has so wide a way to turn,
Has power more than any man may know.
Mine is the drowning in sea below;
Mine is the dungeon underneath the moat;
1605 Mine is the hanging and strangling by the throat;
Rebellion, and the base crowd's murmuring,
The groaning and the private poisoning,
And vengeance and amercement—all are mine,
While yet I dwell within the Lion's sign.[73]
1610 Mine is the ruining of all high halls,
And tumbling down of towers and of walls
Upon the miner and the carpenter.
I struck down Samson, that pillar shaker;
And mine are all the maladies so cold,
1615 The treasons dark, the machinations old;
My glance is father of all pestilence.
Now weep no more. I'll see, with diligence,
That Palamon, who is your own true knight,
Shall have his lady, as you hold is right.
1620 Though Mars may help his man, yet none the less
Between you two there must come sometime peace,
And though you be not of one temperament,
Causing each day such violent dissent,
I am your grandsire and obey your will;
1625 Weep then no more, your pleasure I'll fulfill."
Now will I cease to speak of gods above,
Of Mars and Venus, goddess of all love,
And tell you now, as plainly as I can,
The great result, for which I first began.

[73] *the astrological sign Leo*

1630   *Explicit tercia pars.*
                 Sequitur pars quarta.[74]

Great was the fête[75] in Athens on that day,
And too, the merry season of the May
Gave everyone such joy and such pleasance
1635 That all that Monday they'd but joust and dance,
Or spend the time in Venus' high service.
But for the reason that they must arise
Betimes, to see the heralded great fight,
All they retired to early rest that night.
1640 And on the morrow, when that day did spring,
Of horse and harness, noise and clattering,
There was enough in hostelries about.
And to the palace rode full many a rout
Of lords, bestriding steeds and on palfreys.[76]

1645 There could you see adjusting of harness,
So curious and so rich, and wrought so well
Of goldsmiths' work, embroidery, and of steel;

The shields, the helmets bright, the gay trappings,[77]

The gold-hewn casques,[78] the coats-of-arms, the rings,
1650 The lords in vestments rich, on their coursers,[79]

Knights with their retinues and also squires;
The rivetting of spears, the helm-buckling,
The strapping of the shields, and. thong-lacing-
In their great need, not one of them was idle;
1655 The frothing steeds, champing the golden bridle,
And the quick smiths, and armourers also,
With file and hammer spurring to and fro;
Yeoman, and peasants with short staves were out,
Crowding as thick as they could move about;
1660 Pipes, trumpets, kettledrums, and clarions,[80]
That in the battle sound such grim summons;
The palace full of people, up and down,
Here three, there ten, debating the renown
And questioning about these Theban knights,
1665 Some put it thus, some said, "It's so by rights."
Some held with him who had the great black beard,
Some with the bald-heads, some with the thick haired;
Some said, "He looks grim, and he'll fight like hate;
He has an axe of twenty pound in weight."

1670 And thus the hall was full of gossiping
Long after the bright sun began to spring.
     The mighty Theseus, from sleep awakened
By songs and all the noise that never slackened,
Kept yet the chamber of this rich palace,
1675 Till the two Theban knights, with equal grace
And honour, were ushered in with flourish fitting.
Duke Theseus was at a window sitting,
Arrayed as he were god upon a throne.
Then pressed the people thitherward[81] full soon,
1680 To see him and to do him reverence,
Aye, and to hear commands of sapience.
     A herald on a scaffold cried out "Ho!"
Till all the people's noise was stilled; and so
When he observed that all were fallen still,
1685 He then proclaimed the mighty ruler's will.
"The duke our lord, full wise and full discreet,
Holds that it were but wanton waste to meet
For gentle folk to fight all in the guise
Of mortal battle in this enterprise.
1690 Wherefore, in order that no man may die,
He does his earlier purpose modify.
No man, therefore, on pain of loss of life,
Shall any arrow, pole-axe, or short knife
Send into lists in any wise, or bring;
1695 Nor any shortened sword, for point-thrusting,
Shall a man draw, or bear it by his side.
Nor shall a knight against opponent ride,
Save one full course, with any sharp-ground spear;
Unhorsed, a man may thrust with any gear.
1700 And he that's overcome, should this occur,
Shall not be slain, but brought to barrier,
Whereof there shall be one on either side;
Let him be forced to go there and abide.
And if by chance the leader there must go,
1705 Of either side, or slay his equal foe,
No longer, then, shall tourneying endure.
God speed you; go forth now, and lay on sure.
With long sword and with maces fight your fill.
Go now your ways; this is the lord duke's will."

[80]*trumpets*
[81]*pushed them*

1710   The voices of the people rent the skies,
           Such was the uproar of their merry cries:
           "Now God save such a lord, who is so good
           He will not have destruction of men's blood!"
           Up start the trumpets and make melody.
1715 And to the lists rode forth the company,
           In marshaled[82] ranks, throughout the city large,
           All hung with cloth of gold, and not with serge.[83]
           Full like a lord this noble duke did ride,
           With the two Theban knights on either side;
1720 And, following, rode the queen and Emily,
           And, after, came another company
           Of one and other, each in his degree.
           And thus they went throughout the whole city,
           And to the lists they came, all in good time.
1725 The day was not yet fully come to prime
           When throned was Theseus full rich and high,
           And Queen Hippolyta and Emily,
           While other ladies sat in tiers about.
           Into the seats then pressed the lesser rout.
1730 And westward, through the gate of Mars, right hearty,
           Arcita and the hundred of his party
           With banner red is entering anon;
           And in that self-same moment, Palamon
           Is under Venus, eastward in that place,
1730 With banner white, and resolute of face.
           In all the world, searching it up and down,
           So equal were they all, from heel to crown,
           There were no two such bands in any way.
           For there was no man wise enough to say
1735 How either had of other advantage
           In high repute, or in estate, or age,
           So even were they chosen, as I guess.
           And in two goodly ranks they did then dress.
           And when the name was called of every one,
1740 That cheating in their number might be none,
           Then were the gates closed, and the cry rang loud:
           "Now do your devoir,[84] all you young knights proud!"
           The heralds cease their spurring up and down;
           Now ring the trumpets as the charge is blown;

there
[82]*organized*

[83]*a cheap, woolen fabric*

[84]*duty*

1745   And there's no more to say, for east and west
        Two hundred spears are firmly laid in rest;
        In goes the sharpened spur, into the side.
        Now see men who can joust and who can ride!
        Now shivered are the shafts on bucklers thick;
1750   One feels through very breast-bone the spear's prick;
        Lances are flung full twenty feet in height;
        Out flash the swords like silver burnished bright.
        Helmets are hewed, the lacings rip and shred;
        Out bursts the blood, gushing in stern streams red.
1755   With mighty maces bones are crushed in joust.
        One through the thickest throng begins to thrust.
        There strong steeds stumble now, and down goes all.
        One rolls beneath their feet as rolls a ball.
        One flails about with club, being overthrown,
1760   Another, on a mailed horse, rides him down.
        One through the body's hurt, and led, for aid,
        Despite his protests, to the barricade,
        As compact was, and there he must abide;
        Another's captured by the other side
1765   At times Duke Theseus orders them to rest,
        To eat a bit and drink what each likes best.
        And many times that day those Thebans two
        Met in the fight and wrought each other woe;
        Each has the other unhorsed on that day.
1770   No tigress in the vale of Galgophey,[85]
        Whose little whelp is stolen in the light,
        Is cruel to the hunter as Arcite
        For jealousy is cruel to Palamon;
        Nor in Belmarie,[86] when the hunt is on
1775   Is there a lion, wild for want of food,
        That of his prey desires so much the blood
        As Palamon the death of Arcite there.
        Their jealous blows fall on their helmets fair;
        Out leaps the blood and makes their two sides red.
1780   But sometime comes the end of every deed;
        And ere the sun had sunk to rest in gold,
        The mighty King Emetreus did hold
        This Palamon, as he fought with Arcita,
        And made his sword deep in the flesh to bite;

[85]*a valley in Greece*

[86]*Morocco*

1785 And by the force of twenty men he's made,
    Unyielded, to withdraw to barricade.
    And, trying hard to rescue Palamon,
    The mighty King Lycurgus is borne down;
    And King Emetreus, for all his strength,
1790 Is hurled out of the saddle a sword's length,
    So hits out Palamon once more, or ere
    (But all for naught) he's brought to barrier.
    His hardy heart may now avail him naught;
    He must abide there now, being fairly caught
1795 By force of arms, as by provision known.
        Who sorrows now but woeful Palamon,
    Who may no more advance into the fight?
    And when Duke Theseus had seen this sight,
    Unto the warriors fighting, every one,
1800 He cried out: "Hold! No more! For it is done!
    Now will I prove true judge, of no party.
    Theban Arcita shall have Emily,
    Who, by his fortune, has her fairly won."
    And now a noise of people is begun
1805 For joy of this, so loud and shrill withal,
    It seems as if the very lists will fall.[87]
        But now, what can fair Venus do above?
    What says she now? What does this queen of love
    But weep so fast, for thwarting of her will,
1810 Her tears upon the lists begin to spill.
    She said: "Now am I shamed and over-flung."
    But Saturn said: "My daughter, hold your tongue.
    Mars has his will, his knight has all his boon,
    And, by my head, you shall be eased, and soon."
1815 The trumpeters and other minstrelsy
        The hearalds that did loudly yell and cry,
    Were at their best for joy Sir Arcit.
    But listen now—leave off your noise a bit—
    to the miracle that happened there anon.
1820 This fierce Arcita doffs his helmet soon,
    And mounted on a horse, to show his face,
    He spurs from end to end of that great place,
    Looking aloft to gaze on Emily;
    And she cast down on him a friendly eye

[87] It seemed as though the competition was over.

1825 (For women, generally speaking, go
     Wherever Fortune may her favor show);
     And she was fair to see, and held his heart.
     But from the ground infernal furies start,
     From Pluto sent, at instance of Saturn,
1830 Whereat his horse, for fear, began to turn
     And leap aside, all suddenly falling there;
     And Arcita before he could beware
     Was pitched upon the ground, upon his head
     And lay there, moving not, as he were dead,
1835 So ran the surging blood into his face.
     His chest crushed in upon the saddle-bow.[88]
     And black he lay as ever coal, or crow,
     Anon they carried him from out that place,
     With heavy hearts, to Theseus' palace.

[88]*the arched, front part of the saddle*

1840 There was his harness cut away, each lace,
     And swiftly was he laid upon a bed,
     For he was yet alive and some words said,
     Crying and calling after Emily.
     Duke Theseus, with all his company,
1845 Is come again to Athens, his city,
     With joyous heart and great festivity.
     And though sore grieved for this unhappy fall,
     He would not cast a blight upon them all.
     Men said, too, that Arcita should not die,
1850 But should be healed of all his injury.
     And of another thing they were right fain,
     Which was, that of them all no one was slain,
     Though each was sore, and hurt, and specially one
     Who'd got a lance-head thrust through his breastbone.
1855 For other bruises, wounds and broken arms,
     Some of them carried salves and some had charms;
     And medicines of many herbs, and sage
     They drank, to keep their limbs from hemorrhage.
     In all of which this duke, as he well can,
1860 Now comforts and now honours every man,
     And makes a revelry the livelong night
     For all these foreign lords, as was but right.
     Nor was there held any discomfiting,
     Save from the jousts and from the tourneying.[89]

[89]*participating in tournaments*

1865 For truly, there had been no cause for shame,
     Since being thrown is fortune of the game;
     Nor is it, to be led to barrier,
     Unyielded, and by twenty knights' power,
     One man alone, surrounded by the foe,
1870 Driven by arms, and dragged out, heel and toe,
     And with his courser driven forth with staves
     Of men on foot, yeomen and serving knaves-
     All this imputes to one no kind of vice,
     And no man may bring charge of cowardice.
1875 For which, anon, Duke Theseus bade cry,
     To still all rancour and all keen envy,
     The worth, as well of one side as the other,
     As equal both, and each the other's brother;
     And gave them gifts according to degree,
1880 And held a three days' feast, right royally;
     And then convoyed these kings upon their road
     For one full day, and to them honour showed.
     And home went every man on his right way.
     There was naught more but "Farewell" and "Good-day."
1885 I'll say no more of war, but turn upon
     My tale of Arcita and Palamon.
          Swells now Arcita's breast until the sore
     Increases near his heart yet more and more.
     The clotted blood, in spite of all leech-craft,
1890 Rots in his bulk, and there it must be left,
     Since no device of skillful blood-letting,
     Nor drink of herbs, can help him in this thing.
     The power expulsive, or virtue animal
     Called from its use the virtue natural,
1895 Could not the poison void, nor yet expel.
     The tubes of both his lungs began to swell,
     And every tissue in his breast, and down,
     Is foul with poison and all rotten grown.
     He gains in neither, in his strife to live,
1900 By vomiting or taking laxative;
     All is so broken in that part of him,
     Nature retains no vigour there, nor vim.
     And certainly, where Nature will not work,
     It's farewell physic, bear the man to kirk![90]

[90]church

1905 The sum of all is, Arcita must die,
      And so he sends a word to Emily,
      And Palamon, who was his cousin dear;
      And then he said to them as you shall hear.
      "Naught may the woeful spirit in my heart
1910 Declare one point of how my sorrows smart
      To you, my lady, whom I love the most;
      But I bequeath the service of my ghost
      To you above all others, this being sure
      Now that my life may here no more endure.
1915 Alas, the woe! Alas, the pain so strong
      That I for you have suffered, and so long!
      Alas for death! Alas, my Emily!
      Alas, the parting of our company!
      Alas, my heart's own queen! Alas, my wife!
1920 My soul's dear lady, ender of my life!
      What is this world? What asks a man to have?
      Now with his love, now in the cold dark grave
      Alone, with never any company.
      Farewell, my sweet foe! O my Emily!
1925 Oh, take me in your gentle arms, I pray,
      For love of God, and hear what I will say."
          "I have here, with my cousin Palamon,
      Had strife and rancour many a day that's gone,
      For love of you and for my jealousy.
1930 May Jove so surely guide my soul for me,
      To speak about a lover properly,
      With all the circumstances, faithfully—
      That is to say, truth, honour, and knighthood,
      Wisdom, humility, and kinship good,
1935 And generous soul and all the lover's art—
      So now my Jove[91] have in my soul his part
      In this world, right now, I know of none
      So worthy to be loved as Palamon,
      Who serves you and will do so all his life.
1940 And if you ever should become a wife,
      Forget not Palamon, the noble man."
          And with that word his speech to fail began,
      For from his feet up to his breast had come
      The cold of death, making his body numb.

[91] Jupiter

1945 And furthermore, from his two arms the strength
     Was gone out, now, and he was lost, at length.
     Only the intellect, and nothing more,
     Which dwelt within his heart so sick and sore,
     Began to fail now, when the heart felt death,
1950 And his eyes darkened, and he failed of breath.
     But on his lady turned he still his eye,
     And his last word was, "Mercy, Emily!"
     His spirit changed its house and went from here.
     As I was never there, I can't say where.
1955 So I stop, not being a soothsayer;
     Of souls here naught shall I enregister;[92]
     Nor do I wish their notions, now, to tell
     Who write of them, though they say where they dwell.
     Archita's cold; Mars guides his soul on high;
1960 Now will I speak forthwith of Emily.

          Shrieked Emily and howled now Palamon,
     Till Theseus his sister took, anon,
     And bore her, swooning for the corpse, away.
     How shall it help, to dwell the livelong day
1965 In telling how she wept both night and morrow?
     For in like cases women have such sorrow,
     When their good husband from their side must go,
     And, for the greater part, they take on so,
     Or else they fall into such malady
1970 That, at the last, and certainly, they die.

          Infinite were the sorrows and the tears
     Of all old folk and folk of tender years
     Throughout the town, at death of this Theban;
     For him there wept the child and wept the man;
1975 So great a weeping was not, 'tis certain,
     When Hector was brought back, but newly slain,
     To Troy. Alas, the sorrow that was there!
     Tearing of cheeks and rending out of hair.
     "Oh why will you be dead," these women cry,
1980 "Who had of gold enough, and Emily?"
     No man might comfort then Duke Theseus,
     Excepting his old father, Aegeus,
     Who knew this world's mutations, and men's own,
     Since he had seen them changing up and down,

1985 Joy after woe, and woe from happiness:
He showed them, by example, the process.
     "Just as there never died a man," quoth he,
"But he had lived on earth in some degree,
Just so there never lived a man," he said,
1990 "In all this world, but must be sometime dead.
This world is but a thoroughfare of woe,
And we are pilgrims passing to and fro;
Death is the end of every worldly sore."
And after this, he told them yet much more
1995 To that effect, all wisely to exhort
The people that they should find some comfort.
     Duke Theseus now considered and with care
What place of burial he should prepare
For good Arcita, as it best might be,
2000 And one most worthy of his high degree.
And at the last concluded, hereupon,
That where at first Arcita and Palamon
Had fought for love, with no man else between,
There in that very grove, so sweet and green,
2005 Where he mused on his amorous desires
Complaining of love's hot and flaming fires,
He'd make a pyre and have the funeral.
Accomplished there, and worthily in all.
And so he gave command to hack and hew
2010 The ancient oaks, and lay them straight and true
In split lengths that would kindle well and burn.
His officers, with sure swift feet, they turn
And ride away to do his whole intent.
And after this Duke Theseus straightway sent
2015 For a great bier, and had it all o'er-spread
With cloth of gold, the richest that he had.
Arcita clad he, too, in cloth of gold;
White glove were on his hands where they did fold;
Upon his head a crown of laurel green,
2020 And near his hand a sword both bright and keen.
Then, having bared the dead face on the bier,
The duke so wept, 'twas pitiful to hear.
And, so that folk might see him, one and all,
When it was day he brought them to the hall

2025 Which echoed of their wailing cries anon.
     Then came this woeful Theban, Palamon,
     With fluttery beard and matted, ash-strewn hair,
     All in black clothes wet with his tears; and there,
     Surpassing all in weeping, Emily,
2030 The most affected of the company.
     And so that every several rite should be
     Noble and rich, and suiting his degree,
     Duke Theseus commanded that they bring
     Three horses, mailed in steel all glittering,
2035 And covered with Arcita's armour bright.
     Upon these stallions, which were large and white,
     There rode three men, whereof one bore the shield.
     And one the spear he'd known so well to wield;
     The third man bore his Turkish bow, nor less
2040 Of burnished gold the quiver than harness;
     And forth they slowly rode, with mournful cheer,
     Toward that grove, as you shall further hear.
          The noblest Greeks did gladly volunteer
     To bear upon their shoulders that great bier,
2045 With measured pace and eyes gone red and wet,
     Through all the city, by the wide main street,
     Which was all spread with black, and, wondrous high,
     Covered with this same cloth were houses nigh.
     Upon the right hand went old Aegeus,
2050 And on the other side Duke Theseus,
     With vessels in their hands, of gold right fine,
     All filled with honey, milk, and blood, and wine;
     And Palamon with a great company;
     And after that came woeful Emily,
2055 With fire in hands, as use was, to ignite
     The sacrifice and set the pyre alight.
          Great labour and full great apparelling
     Went to the service and the fire-making.
     For to the skies that green pyre reached its top,
2060 And twenty fathoms did the arms out-crop,
     That is to say, the branches were so broad.
     Of straw there first was laid full many a load.
     But how the fire was made to climb so high;
     Or what names all the different trees went by,

2065 As oak, fir, birch, asp, alder, poplar, holm
Willow, plane, ash, box, chestnut, linden, elm
Laurel, thorn, maple, beech, yew, dogwood tree,
Or how they were felled, shan't be told by me.
Nor how the wood-gods scampered up and down,

2070 Driven from homes that they had called their own,
Wherein they'd lived so long at ease, in peace,
The nymphs, the fauns,[93] the hamadryades;[94]
Nor how the beasts, for fear, and the birds, all
Fled, when that ancient wood began to fall;

2075 Nor how aghast[95] the ground was in the light,
Not being used to seeing the sun so bright;
Nor how the fire was started first with straw,
And then dry sticks cut into thirds by a saw,
And then with green wood and with spicery,[96]

2080 And then with cloth of gold and jewelery
And garlands hanging with full many a flower,
And myrrh, and incense, sweet as rose in bower;
Nor how Arcita lies among all this,
Nor what vast wealth about his body is;

2085 Nor how this Emily, as was their way,
Lighted the sacred funeral fire, that day,
Nor how she swooned when men built up the fire,
Nor what she said, nor what was her desire;
No, nor what gems men on the fire then cast,

2090 When the white flame went high and burned so fast;
Nor how one cast his shield, and one his spear,
And some their vestments,[97] on that burning bier,
With cups of wine, and cups of milk, and blood,
Into that flame, which burned as wild-fire would;

2095 Nor how the Greeks, in one huge wailing rout,
Rode slowly three times all the fire about,
Upon the left hand, with a loud shouting,
And three times more, with weapons clattering,
While thrice the women there raised up a cry;

2100 Nor how was homeward led sad Emily;
Nor how Arcita burned to ashes cold;
Nor aught of how the lichwake[98] they did hold
All that same night, nor how the Greeks did play[99]
Who, naked, wrestled best, with oil anointed,

[93] *a mythical creature with the body of a man and the legs of a goat*

[94] *the spirit of a tree*

[95] *pale*

[96] *Fine oils and spices were thrown onto funeral fires.*

[97] *clothes*

[98] *a wake or vigil for the dead*

[99] *The ancient Greeks observed major funerals by holding athletic games.*

2105 Nor who best bore himself in deeds appointed.
      I will not even tell how they were gone
      Home, into Athens, when the play was done;
      But briefly to the point, now, will I wend
      And make of this, my lengthy tale, an end.
2110   With passing in their length of certain years,
      All put by was the mourning and the tears
      Of Greeks, as by one general assent;
      And then it seems there was a parliament
      At Athens, upon certain points in case;
2115 Among the which points spoken of there was
      The ratifying of alliances
      That should hold Thebes from all defiances.
      Whereat this noble Theseus, anon,
      Invited there the gentle Palamon,
2120 Not telling him what was the cause and why;
      But in his mourning clothes, and sorrowfully,
      He came upon that bidding, so say I.
      And then Duke Theseus sent for Emily.
      When they were seated and was hushed the place,
2125 And Theseus had mused a little space,
      Ere any word came from his full wise breast,
      His two eyes fixed on whoso pleased him best,
      Then with a sad face sighed he deep and still,
      And after that began to speak his will.
2130   "The Primal Mover and the Cause above,
      When first God forged the goodly chain of love,
      Great the effect, and high was His intent;
      Well knew He why, and what thereof He meant;
      For with that goodly chain of love He bound
2135 The fire, the air, the water, and dry ground
      In certain bounds, the which they might not flee;
      That same First Cause and Mover,"[100] then quoth he,
      "Has stablished in this base world, up and down,
      A certain length of days to call their own
2140 For all that are engendered in this place,
      Beyond the which not one day may they pace,
      Though yet all may that certain time abridge;
      Authority there needs none, I allege,
      For it is well proved by experience,

[100]God

2145 Save that I please to clarify my sense.
Then may men by this order well discern
This Mover to be stable and eterne.
Well may man know, unless he be a fool
That every part derives but from the whole,
2150 For Nature has not taken his being
From any part and portion of a thing,
But from a substance perfect, stable aye,
And so continuing till changed away.
And therefore, of His Wisdom's Providence,
2155 Has He so well established ordinance
That species of all things and all progressions,
If they'd endure, it must be by successions,
Not being themselves eternal, 'tis no lie:
This may you understand and see by eye."
2160   "Lo now, the oak, that has long nourishing
Even from the time that it begins to spring,
And has so long a life, as we may see,
Yet at the last all wasted is the tree.
"Consider, too, how even the hard stone
2165 Under our feet we tread each day upon
Yet wastes it, as it lies beside the way.
And the broad river will be dry some day.
And great towns wane; we see them vanishing.
Thus may we see the end to everything."
2170   "Of man and woman just the same is true:
Needs must, in either season of the two,
That is to say, in youth or else in age,
All men perish, the king as well as page;
Some in their bed, and some in the deep sea,
2175 And some in the wide field—as it may be;
There's naught will help; all go the same way. Aye,
Then may I say that everything must die.
Who causes this but Jupiter the King?
He is the Prince and Cause of everything,
2180 Converting all back to that primal well
From which it was derived, 'tis sooth to tell.
And against this, for every thing alive,
Of any state, avails it not to strive.
    "Then is it wisdom, as it seems to me,

2185 To make a virtue of necessity,
      And calmly take what we may not eschew,
      And specially that which to all is due.
      Whoso would balk at aught, he does folly,
      And thus rebels against His potency.
2190 And certainly a man has most honour
      In dying in his excellence and flower,
      When he is certain of his high good name;
      For then he gives to friend, and self, no shame.
      And gladder ought a friend be of his death
2195 When, in much honour, he yields up his breath,
      Than when his name's grown feeble with old age;
      For all forgotten, then, is his courage.
      Hence it is best for all of noble name
      To die when at the summit of their fame.
2200 The contrary of this is wilfulness.
      Why do we grumble? Why have heaviness
      That good Arcita, chivalry's fair flower,
      Is gone, with honour, in his best-lived hour,
      Out of the filthy prison of this life?
2205 Why grumble here his cousin and his wife
      About his welfare, who loved them so well?
      Can he thank them? Nay, God knows, not! Nor tell
      How they his soul and their own selves offend."
      Though yet they may not their desires amend.
2210   "What may I prove by this long argument
      Save that we all turn to merriment,
      After our grief, and give Jove thanks for grace.
      And so, before we go from out this place,
      I counsel that we make, of sorrows two,
2215 One perfect joy, lasting for aye, for you;
      And look you now, where most woe is herein,
      There will we first amend it and begin.
          "Sister," quoth he, "you have my full consent,
      With the advice of this my Parliament,
2220 That gentle Palamon, your own true knight,
      Who serves you well with will and heart and might,
      And so has ever, since you knew him first—
      That you shall, of your grace, allay his thirst
      By taking him for husband and for lord:

2225 Lend me your hand, for this is our accord.
     Let now your woman's pity make him glad.
     For he is a king's brother's son, by gad;
     And though he were a poor knight bachelor,
     Since he has served you for so many a year,
2230 And borne for you so great adversity,
     This ought to weigh with you, it seems to me,
     For mercy ought to dominate mere right."
         Then said he thus to Palamon the knight:
     "I think there needs but little sermoning
2235 To make you give consent, now, to this thing.
     Come near, and take your lady by the hand."
     Between them, then, was tied that nuptial band,
     Which is called matrimony or marriage,
     By all the council and the baronage.
2240 And thus, in all bliss and with melody,
     Has Palamon now wedded Emily.
     And God, Who all this universe has wrought,
     Send him His love, who has it dearly bought.
     For now has Palamon, in all things, wealth,
2245 Living in bliss, in riches, and in health;
     And Emily loved him so tenderly,
     And he served her so well and faithfully,
     That never word once marred their happiness,
     No jealousy, nor other such distress.
2250 Thus ends now Palamon and Emily;
     And may God save all this fair company! Amen.

The
Miller's
P R O L O G U E

WHEN THAT THE Knight had thus his story told,
In all the crowd there was not young or old
Who didn't say it was a noble story
And worthy to be called into memory.
5 The high-born ones, especially, felt this way.
Our host did laugh and swear, "So I daresay,
This goes quite well; unbuckled is the sack.
Let's see now who shall give a story back.
For certainly the game is well began.
10 Now tell to us, Sir Monk, if that you can
Something to measure up to the Knight's tale."
The Miller, drunk enough to be all pale,
So that barely upon his horse he sat,
He would not lower neither hood nor hat,
15 Nor wait for any out of courtesy,
But in the voice of Pilate[1] 'gan to cry,
And then he swore, "By arms, by bones and blood,
I know a noble story for this crowd,
With which I will now equal the Knight's tale."
20 Our Host saw that the monk was drunk on ale,
And said, "Hold off awhile, Robyn, dear brother;
Some better man shall first tell us another.

[1] i.e., a loud voice, like the character of Pilate in medieval religious plays

Hold off, and let us do this properly."
"By soul of God,"said he, "that will not I;
25 For I will speak, or else go on my way."
Our Host answered, "Tell on, by devil's way!
You are a fool; your wit is overcome."
"Now hearken," said the Miller, "all and some—
But first I make the protest all around
30 That I am drunk; I know it by my sound.
And therefore if I misspeak or missay,
Blame that on ale of Southwark, I you pray.
For I will tell a legend and a life
Both of a carpenter and of his wife,
35 How that a clerk hath set the woodwright's cap."
The Reeve answered and said, "Stop your claptrap!
Let be your lewd and drunken harlotry.
It is a sin and also great folly
To injure any man, or him defame,
40 And to bring wives into this kind of fame.
You have enough of other tales to spin."
This drunken miller spoke full soon again
And said, "My dearest brother Osewold,
A man who has no wife is no cuckold.
45 But I say not that therefore you are one;
There have been quite good women, many a one,
And ever a thousand good against one bad.
You know this well yourself, unless you're mad.
Why are you angry with my story now?
50 I have a wife, by God, as well as thou;
Yet won't I, for the oxen at my trough,
Take on more than I know to be enough
And say about myself that I am one;
I will believe truly that I am none.
55 A husband shall not be inquisitive
Of God's secrets, nor how his woman lives.
As long as he finds God's plenty in her,
Of all the rest he needs not to inquire."
What have I more to say, but this miller
60 Would not his words for any man defer,
But told his boorish tale in his own style.
I feel regret repeating it this while.

And therefore, every proper man, I pray,
For love of God, do not take what I say
65 As meant in evil, for I must rehearse
All of their tales, be they better or worse.
For if I don't, I'm false to my subject.
And therefore, anyone who might object,
Now turn the page and choose another tale;
70 For he shall find enough, both great and small,
Of history that deals with nobleness,
And, too, morality and holiness.
And don't blame me if you should choose amiss.
The Miller is a churl,[2] you well know this.
75 So was the Reeve also and others too,
And harlotry was in their stories two.
Advise yourself, and put me out of blame,
For men should not make earnest of a game.

[2]*a rude, coarse man*

The
Miller's
T A L E

ONCE ON A TIME was dwelling in Oxford
A wealthy lout[1] who took in guests to board,
And of his craft he was a carpenter.
A poor scholar was lodging with him there,

5 Who'd learned the arts, but all his fantasy[2]
Was turned to study of astrology;
And knew a certain set of theorems
And could find out by various strategems,
If men but asked of him in certain hours

10 When they should have a drought or else have showers,
Or if men asked of him what should befall
To anything—I cannot list them all.
    This clerk was called the clever Nicholas;
Of secret loves he knew and their solace;

15 And he kept counsel, too, for he was sly
And meek as any maiden passing by.
He had a chamber in that hostelry,
And lived alone there, with no company,
All garnished with sweet herbs of good repute;

20 And he himself sweet-smelling as the root
Of licorice, valerian, or setwall.[3]
His *Almagest*,[4] and books both great and small

[1]*brute*

[2]*hobby*

[3]*sweet herbs*
[4]*book on astrology*

97

⁵*an instrument used to calculate the positions of stars and planets*

⁶*counting stones*

⁷*harp*

⁸*a medieval carol*

⁹*a popular tune*

¹⁰*a man cheated on by his wife*

¹¹*a Roman writer often cited by medieval authors*

¹²*flare*

¹³*headband*

¹⁴*lecherous*

¹⁵*a fruit related to a plum*

His astrolabe,⁵ belonging to his art,
His algorism stones⁶—all laid apart
25 On shelves that ranged beside his lone bed's head;
His press was covered with a cloth of red.
And over all there lay a psaltery⁷
Whereon he made an evening's melody,
Playing so sweetly that the chamber rang;
30 And *Angelus ad virginem*⁸ he sang;
And after that he warbled the *King's Note:*⁹
Often in good voice was his merry throat.
And thus this gentle clerk his leisure spends
Supported by some income and his friends.
35   This carpenter had lately wed a wife
Whom he loved better than he loved his life;
And she was come to eighteen years of age.
Jealous he was and held her close in cage.
For she was wild and young and he was old,
40 And deemed himself as like to be cuckold.¹⁰
He knew not Cato,¹¹ for his lore was rude:
That vulgar man should wed similitude.
A man should wed according to estate,
For youth and age are often in debate.
45 But now, since he had fallen in the snare,
He must endure, like other folk, his care.
    Fair was this youthful wife, and therewithal
As weasel's was her body slim and small.
A girdle wore she, barred and striped, of silk.
50 An apron, too, as white as morning milk
About her loins, and full of many a gore;¹²
White was her smock, embroidered all before
And even behind, her collar round about,
Of coal-black silk, on both sides, in and out;
55 The strings of the white cap upon her head
Were, like her collar, black silk worked with thread;
Her fillet¹³ was of wide silk worn full high:
And certainly she had a lickerish¹⁴ eye.
She'd thinned out carefully her eyebrows two,
60 And they were arched and black as any sloe.¹⁵
She was a far more pleasant thing to see
Than is the newly budded young pear-tree;

The
Miller's
T A L E

ONCE ON A TIME was dwelling in Oxford
A wealthy lout[1] who took in guests to board,
And of his craft he was a carpenter.
A poor scholar was lodging with him there,
5 Who'd learned the arts, but all his fantasy[2]
Was turned to study of astrology;
And knew a certain set of theorems
And could find out by various strategems,
If men but asked of him in certain hours
10 When they should have a drought or else have showers,
Or if men asked of him what should befall
To anything—I cannot list them all.
　　This clerk was called the clever Nicholas;
Of secret loves he knew and their solace;
15 And he kept counsel, too, for he was sly
And meek as any maiden passing by.
He had a chamber in that hostelry,
And lived alone there, with no company,
All garnished with sweet herbs of good repute;
20 And he himself sweet-smelling as the root
Of licorice, valerian, or setwall.[3]
His *Almagest*,[4] and books both great and small

[1]*brute*

[2]*hobby*

[3]*sweet herbs*
[4]*book on astrology*

97

His astrolabe,[5] belonging to his art,
His algorism stones[6]—all laid apart
25 On shelves that ranged beside his lone bed's head;
His press was covered with a cloth of red.
And over all there lay a psaltery[7]
Whereon he made an evening's melody,
Playing so sweetly that the chamber rang;
30 And *Angelus ad virginem*[8] he sang;
And after that he warbled the *King's Note*:[9]
Often in good voice was his merry throat.
And thus this gentle clerk his leisure spends
Supported by some income and his friends.
35   This carpenter had lately wed a wife
Whom he loved better than he loved his life;
And she was come to eighteen years of age.
Jealous he was and held her close in cage.
For she was wild and young and he was old,
40 And deemed himself as like to be cuckold.[10]
He knew not Cato,[11] for his lore was rude:
That vulgar man should wed similitude.
A man should wed according to estate,
For youth and age are often in debate.
45 But now, since he had fallen in the snare,
He must endure, like other folk, his care.
    Fair was this youthful wife, and therewithal
As weasel's was her body slim and small.
A girdle wore she, barred and striped, of silk.
50 An apron, too, as white as morning milk
About her loins, and full of many a gore;[12]
White was her smock, embroidered all before
And even behind, her collar round about,
Of coal-black silk, on both sides, in and out;
55 The strings of the white cap upon her head
Were, like her collar, black silk worked with thread;
Her fillet[13] was of wide silk worn full high:
And certainly she had a lickerish[14] eye.
She'd thinned out carefully her eyebrows two,
60 And they were arched and black as any sloe.[15]
She was a far more pleasant thing to see
Than is the newly budded young pear-tree;

[5]*an instrument used to calculate the positions of stars and planets*

[6]*counting stones*

[7]*harp*

[8]*a medieval carol*

[9]*a popular tune*

[10]*a man cheated on by his wife*

[11]*a Roman writer often cited by medieval authors*

[12]*flare*

[13]*headband*

[14]*lecherous*

[15]*a fruit related to a plum*

And softer than the wool is on a wether.[16]
Down from her girdle hung a purse of leather,

[16]*ram*

65 Tasselled with silk, with latten[17] beading sown.

[17]*brass*

In all this world, searching it up and down,
So gay a little doll, I well believe,
Or such a wench, there's no man can conceive.
Far brighter was the brilliance of her hue
70 Than in the Tower[18] the gold coins minted new.

[18]*Tower of London*

And songs came shrilling from her pretty head
As from a swallow's sitting on a shed.
Therewith she'd dance too, and could play and sham
Like any kid or calf about its dam.[19]

[19]*mother*

75 Her mouth was sweet as bragget[20] or as mead

[20]*honeyed ale*

Or hoard of apples laid in hay or weed.
Skittish she was as is a pretty colt,
Tall as a staff and straight as cross-bow bolt.
A brooch she wore upon her collar low,
80 As broad as boss of buckler did it show;
Her shoes laced up to where a girl's legs thicken.
She was a primrose, and a tender chicken
For any lord to lay upon his bed,
Or yet for any good yeoman to wed.
85   Now, sir, and then, sir, so befell the case,
That on a day this clever Nicholas
Fell in with this young wife to toy and play,
The while he husband was down Osney way,
Clerks being as crafty as the best of us;
90 And unperceived he caught her by the puss,
Saying: "Indeed, unless I have my will,
For secret love of you, sweetheart, I'll spill."[21]

[21]*die*

And held her hard about the hips, and how!—
And said: "O darling, love me, love me now,
95 Or I shall die, and pray that God me save!"
    And she leaped as a colt does in the trave,[22]

[22]*a pen in which a colt is kept when being fitted for shoes*

And with her head she twisted fast away,
And said: "I will not kiss you, by my fay!
Why, let go," cried she, "let go, Nicholas!
100 Or I will call for help and cry 'alas!'
Do take your hands away, for courtesy!"
    This Nicholas for mercy then did cry,

And spoke so well, and pressed his cause so fast
that she her love did grant him at the last,
105 And swore her oath, by Saint Thomas of Kent,[23]
that she would be at his command, content,
As soon as opportunity she could spy.
    "My husband is so full of jealousy,
Unless you will await me secretly,
110 I know I'm just as good as dead," said she.
    "You must keep all quite hidden in this case."
        "Nay, thereof worry not," said Nicholas,
"A clerk has lazily employed his while
If he cannot a carpenter beguile."
115   And thus they were agreed, and then they swore
To wait a while, as I have said before.
When Nicholas had done thus every whit
And patted her about the loins a bit,
He kissed her sweetly, took his psaltery,
120 And played it fast and made a melody.
        Then fell it thus, that to the parish kirk,[24]
The Lord Christ Jesus' own works for to work,
This good wife went, upon a holy day;
Her forehead shone as bright as does the May,
125 So well she'd washed it when she left off work.
        Now there was of that church a parish clerk
The which that bore the name of Absalom.
Curled was his hair, shining like gold, and from
His head spread fanwise in a thick bright mop;
130 'Twas parted straight and even on the top;
His cheek was red, his eyes grey as a goose;
With Saint Paul's[25] windows cut upon his shoes,
He stood in red hose fitting famously.
And he was clothed full well and properly
135 All in a coat of blue, in which were let
Holes for the lacings, which were fairly set.
And over all he wore a fine surplice[26]
As white as ever hawthorn spray, and nice.
A merry lad he was, so God me save,
140 And well could he let blood, cut hair, and shave,[27]
And draw a deed or quitclaim,[28] as might chance.
In twenty manners could he trip and dance,

---

[23]*Thomas à Becket*

[24]*church*

[25]*Saint Paul's Cathedral, in London*

[26]*church garment*

[27]*duties often performed by clerks*

[28]*a legal document*

After the school that reigned in Oxford,[29] though,
And with his two legs swinging to and fro;

145 And he could play upon a violin;
Thereto he sang in treble voice and thin;
And as well could he play on the guitar.
In all the town no inn was, and no bar,
That he'd not visited to make good cheer,

150 Especially were lively barmaids there.
But, truth to tell, he was a bit squeamish
Of farting and of language haughtyish.

This Absalom, who was so light and gay,
Went with a censer[30] on the holy day,

155 Censing the wives like an enthusiast;
And on them many a loving look he cast,
Especially on this carpenter's goodwife.
To look at her he thought a merry life,
She was so pretty, sweet, and lickerous.

160 I dare well say, if she had been a mouse
And he a cat, he would have mauled her some.

This parish clerk, this lively Absalom
Had in his heart, now, such a love-longing
That from no wife took he an offering;

165 For courtesy, he said, he would take none.
The moon, when it was night, full brightly shone,
And his guitar did Absalom then take,
For in love-watching he'd intent to wake.
And forth he went, jolly and amorous,

170 Until he came unto the carpenter's house
A little after cocks began to crow;
And took his stand beneath a shot-window[31]
That was let into the good wood-wright's wall.
He sang then, in his pleasant voice and small,

175 "Oh now, dear lady, if your will it be,
I pray that you will have some ruth[32] on me,"
The words in harmony with his string-plucking.
This carpenter awoke and heard him sing,
And called unto his wife and said, in sum:

180 "What, Alison! Do you hear Absalom,
Who plays and sings beneath our bedroom wall?"
And she said to her husband, therewithal:

[29] *the oldest university in England*

[30] *a container for burning church incense*

[31] *shuttered window*

[32] *pity*

"Yes, God knows, John, I hear it, truth to tell."
        So this went on; what is there better than well?
185 From day to day this pretty Absalom
     So wooed her he was woebegone therefrom.
     He lay awake all night and all the day;
     He combed his spreading hair and dressed him gay;
     By go-betweens and agents, too, wooed he,
190 And swore her loyal page he'd ever be.
     He sang as tremulously as nightingale;
     He sent her sweetened wine and well-spiced ale
     And waffles piping hot out of the fire,
     And, she being town-bred, mead for her desire.
195 For some by tricks, and some by long descent.
     Once, to display his versatility,

[33] a character in a
medieval religious
play

     He acted Herod[33] on a scaffold high.
          But what availed it him in any case?
     She was enamoured so of Nicholas
200 That Absalom might go and blow his horn;
     He got naught for his labour but her scorn.
     And thus she made of Absalom her ape,

[34] joke

     And all his earnestness she made a jape.[34]
     For truth is in this proverb, and no lie,
205 Men say well thus: It's always he that's nigh
     That makes the absent lover seem a sloth.
     For now, though Absalom be wildly wroth,
     Because he is so far out of her sight,
     This handy Nicholas stands in his light.
210   Now bear you well, you clever Nicholas!
     For Absalom may wail and sing "Alas!"
     And so it chanced that on a Saturday
     This carpenter departed to Osney;
     And clever Nicholas and Alison

[35] trick

215 Were well agreed to this effect: anon
     This Nicholas should put in play a wile[35]
     The simple, jealous husband to beguile;
     And if it chanced the game should go a-right,
     She was to sleep within his arms all night,
220 For this was his desire, and hers also.
     Presently then, and without more ado,
     This Nicholas, no longer did he tarry,

But softly to his chamber did he carry
Both food and drink to last at least a day,
225 Saying that to her husband she should say—
If he should come to ask for Nicholas—
Why, she should say she knew not where he was,
For all day she'd not seen him, far or nigh;
She thought he must have got some malady,
230 Because in vain her maid would knock and call;
He'd answer not, whatever might befall.
    And so it was that all that Saturday
This Nicholas quietly in chamber lay,
And ate and slept, or did what pleased him best,
235 Till Sunday when the sun had gone to rest.
    This simple man with wonder heard the tale,
And marvelled what their Nicholas might ail,
And said: "I am afraid, by Saint Thomas,
That everything's not well with Nicholas.
240 God send he be not dead so suddenly!
This world is most unstable, certainly;
I saw, today, the corpse being borne to kirk
Of one who, but last Monday, was at work.
Go up," said he unto his boy anon,
245 "Call at his door, or knock there with a stone,
Learn how it is and boldly come tell me."
    The servant went up, then, right sturdily,
And at the chamber door, the while he stood,
He cried and knocked as any madman would—
250 "What! How! What do you, Master Nicholay?
How can you sleep through all the livelong day?"
    But all for naught, he never heard a word;
A hole he found, low down upon a board,
Through which the house cat had been wont to creep;
255 And to that hole he stooped, and through did peep,
And finally he ranged him in his sight.
This Nicholas sat gaping there, upright,
As if he'd looked too long at the new moon.
Downstairs he went and told his master soon
260 In what array he'd found this self-same man.
    This carpenter to cross himself began,
And said: "Now help us, holy Frideswide!³⁶

³⁶*the patron saint of Oxford*

Little a man can know what shall betide.
This man is fallen, with his astromy,
265 Into some madness or some agony;
I always feared that somehow this would be!
Men should not meddle in God's privity.
Aye, blessed always be the ignorant man,
Whose creed is all he ever has to scan!
270 So fared another clerk with astromy;
He walked into the meadows for to pry
Into the stars, to learn what should befall,
Until into a clay-pit he did fall;
He saw not that. But yet, by Saint Thomas,
275 I'm sorry for this clever Nicholas.
He shall be scolded for his studying,
If not too late, by Jesus, Heaven's King!
        "Get me a staff, that I may pry before,
The while you, Robin, heave against the door.
280 We'll take him from this studying, I guess."
        And on the chamber door, then, he did press.
His servant was a stout lad, if a dunce,
And by the hasp he heaved it up at once;
Upon the floor that portal fell anon.
285 This Nicholas sat there as still as stone,
Gazing, with gaping mouth, straight up in air.
This carpenter thought he was in despair,
And took him by the shoulders, mightily,
And shook him hard, and cried out, vehemently:
290 "What! Nicholay! Why how now! Come, look down!
Awake, and think on Jesus' death and crown!
I cross you from all elves and magic wights!"
        And then the night-spell[37] said he out, by rights,
At the four corners of the house about,
295 And at the threshold of the door, without:—
        "O Jesus Christ and good Saint Benedict,
Protect this house from all that may afflict,
For the night hag the white Paternoster![38]—
Where hast thou gone, Saint Peter's sister?"
300 And at the last this clever Nicholas
Began to sigh full sore, and said: "Alas!
Shall all the world be lost so soon again?"

[37]a spell to cast out dark spirits

[38]usually the Lord's Prayer; in this case, a prayer used to drive out spirits

This carpenter replied: "What say you, then?
What! Think on God, as we do, men that swink."[39]

39*toil*

305   This Nicholas replied: "Go fetch me drink;
And afterward I'll tell you privately
A certain thing concerning you and me;
I'll tell it to no other man or men."
       This carpenter went down and came again,
310 And brought of potent ale a brimming quart;
And when each one of them had drunk his part,
Nicholas shut the door fast, and with that
He drew a seat and near the carpenter sat.
       He said: "Now, John, my good host, lief[40] and dear,

40*beloved*

315 You must upon your true faith swear, right here,
That to no man will you this word betray;
For it is Christ's own word that I will say,
And if you tell a man, you're ruined quite;
This punishment shall come to you, of right,
320 That if you're traitor you'll go mad—and should!"
       "Nay, Christ forbid it, for His holy blood!"
Said then this simple man: "I am no blab,
Nor, though I say it, am I fond of gab.
Say what you will, I never will it tell
325 To child or wife, by Him that harried[41] Hell!"

41*Jesus*

       "Now, John," said Nicholas, "I will not lie;
But I've found out, from my astrology,
As I have looked upon the moon so bright,
That now, come Monday next, at nine of night,
330 Shall fall a rain so wildly mad as would
Have been, by half, greater than Noah's flood.
This world," he said, "in less time than an hour,
Shall all be drowned, so terrible is this shower;
Thus shall all mankind drown and lose all life."
335   This carpenter replied: "Alas, my wife!
And shall she drown? Alas, my Alison!"
For grief of this he almost fell. Anon
He said: "Is there no remedy in this case?"
       "Why yes, good luck," said clever Nicholas,
340 "If you will work by counsel of the wise;
You must not act on what your wits advise.
For so says Solomon,[42] and it's all true,

42*a wise king in
the Bible*

[43]*regret*

[44]*in the Bible, a man told by God to build a boat in preparation for a great flood*

'Work by advice and thou shalt never rue.'[43]
And if you'll act as counselled and not fail,
345 I undertake, without a mast or sail,
To save us all, aye you and her and me.
Haven't you heard of Noah,[44] how saved was he,
Because Our Lord had warned him how to keep
Out of the flood that covered earth so deep?"
350   "Yes," said the carpenter, "long years ago."
     "Have you not heard," asked Nicholas, "also
The sorrow of Noah and his fellowship
In getting his wife to go aboard the ship?
He would have rather, I dare undertake,
355 At that time, and for all the weather black,
That she had one ship for herself alone.
Therefore, do you know what would best be done?
This thing needs haste, and of a hasty thing
Men must not preach nor do long tarrying.
360   "Presently go, and fetch here to this inn
A kneading-tub, or brewing vat, and win
One each for us, but see that they are large,
Wherein we may swim out as in a barge,
And have therein sufficient food and drink
365 For one day only; that's enough, I think.
The water will dry up and flow away

[45]*nine a.m.*

About the prime[45] of the succeeding day.
But Robin must not know of this, your knave,
And even Jill, your maid, I may not save;
370 Ask me not why, for though you do ask me,
I will not tell you of God's privity.
Suffice you, then, unless your wits are mad,
To have a great a grace as Noah had.
Your wife I shall not lose, there is no doubt,
375 Go, now, your way, and speedily get about,
But when you have, for you and her and me,
Procured these kneading-tubs, or beer-vats, three,
Then you shall hang them near the roof-tree high,

[46]*preparation*

That no man our purveyance[46] may espy.
380 And when you thus have done, as I have said,
And have put in our drink and meat and bread,
Also an axe to cut the ropes in two

When the flood comes, that we may float and go,
And cut a hole, high up, upon the gable,
385 Upon the garden side, over the stable,
That we may freely pass forth on our way
When the great rain and flood are gone that day—
Then shall you float as merrily, I'll stake,
As does the white duck after the white drake.
390 Then I will call, 'Ho, Alison! Ho, John!
Be cheery, for the flood will pass anon.'
And you will say, 'Hail, Master Nicholay!
Good morn, I see you well, for it is day!'
And then shall we be barons all our life
395 Of all the world, like Noah and his wife.
    "But of one thing I warn you now, outright.
Be well advised, that on that very night
When we have reached our ships and got aboard,
Not one of us must speak or whisper word,
400 Nor call, nor cry, but sit in silent prayer;
For this is God's own bidding, hence—don't dare!
    "Your wife and you must hang apart, that in
The night shall come no chance for you to sin
Either in looking or in carnal deed.
405 These orders I have told you, go, God speed!
Tomorrow night, when all men are asleep,
Into our kneading-tubs will we three creep
And sit there, still, awaiting God's high grace.
Go, now, your way, I have no longer space
410 Of time to make a longer sermoning.
Men say thus: 'Send the wise and say no thing.'
You are so wise it needs not that I teach;
Go, save our lives, and that I do beseech."
    This sill carpenter went on his way.
415 Often he cried "Alas!" and "Welaway!"
And to his wife he told all, privately;
But she was better taught thereof than he
How all this rigmarole[47] was to apply.
Nevertheless she acted as she'd die,
420 And said: "Alas! Go on your way anon,
Help us escape, or we are lost, each one;
I am your true and lawfully wedded wife;

[47] *ridiculous action*

Go, my dear spouse, and help to save our life."
Lo, what a great thing is affection found!
425 Men die of imagination, I'll be bound,
So deep an imprint may the spirit take.
This hapless carpenter began to quake;
He thought now, verily, that he could see
Old Noah's flood come wallowing like the sea
430 To drown his Alison, his honey dear.
He wept, he wailed, he made but sorry cheer,
He sighed and made full many a sob and sough.
He went and got himself a kneading-trough
And, after that, two tubs he somewhere found
435 And to his dwelling privately sent round,
And hung them near the roof, all secretly.
With his own hand, then, made he ladders three,
To climb up by the rungs thereof, it seems,
And reach the tubs left hanging to the beams;

48stocked with food   440 And those he victualled[48] tubs and kneading-trough
With bread and cheese and good jugged ale, enough
To satisfy the needs of one full day.
But ere he'd put all this in such array,
He sent his servants, boy and maid, right down
445 Upon some errand into London town.
And on the Monday, when it came on night,
He shut his door, without a candle-light,
And ordered everything as it should be.
And shortly after up they climbed, all three;

49about 660 feet   450 They sat while one might plow a furlong-way.[49]
"Now, by Our Father, hush!" said Nicholay,
And "Hush!" said John, and "Hush!" said Alison.
This carpenter, his loud devotion done,
Sat silent, saying mentally a prayer,
455 And waiting for the rain, to hear it there.
The deathlike sleep of utter weariness
Fell on this wood-wright even (as I guess)
About the curfew time, or little more;

50effort   For travail[50] of his spirit he groaned sore,
460 And soon he snored, for badly his head lay.
Down by the ladder crept his Nicholay,
And Alison, right softly down she sped.

Without more words they went and got in bed
Even where the carpenter was wont[51] to lie.
465   There was the revel and the melody!
And thus lie Alison and Nicholas,
In joy that goes by many an alias,
Until the bells for lauds[52] began to ring
And friars to the chancel[53] went to sing.
470   This parish clerk, this amorous Absalom,
Whom love has made so woebegone and dumb,
Upon the Monday was down Osney way,
With company, to find some sport and play;
And there he chanced to ask a cloisterer,
475   Privately, after John the carpenter.
This monk drew him apart, out of the kirk,[54]
And said: "I have not seen him here at work
Since Saturday; I think well that he went
For timber, that the abbot has him sent;
480   For he is wont for timber thus to go,
Remaining at the grange[55] a day or so;
Or else he's surely at his house today;
But which it is I cannot truly say."
        This Absalom right happy was and light,
485   And thought: "Now is the time to wake all night;
For certainly I saw him not stirring
About his door since day began to spring.
So may I thrive, as I shall, at cock's crow,
Knock cautiously upon the window low
490   Which is so placed upon his bedroom wall.
To Alison then will I tell of all
My love-longing, and thus I shall not miss
That at the least I'll have her lips to kiss.
Some sort of comfort shall I have, I say,
495   My mouth's been itching all this livelong day;
That is a sign of kissing at the least.
Al night I dreamed, too, I was at a feast.
Therefore I'll go and sleep two hours away,
And all this night then will I wake and play."
500   And so when time of first cock-crow was come,
Up rose this merry lover, Absalom,
And dressed him gay and all at point-device,[56]

[51]*used*

[52]*a pre-dawn church service*

[53]*the part of a church containing the choir seats and altar*

[54]*church*

[55]*the outer area of a farm*

[56]*carefully; to the last detail*

But first he chewed some licorice and spice
So he'd smell sweet, ere he had combed his hair.

505 Under his tongue some bits of true-love[57] rare,
For thereby thought he to be more gracious.
He went, then, to the carpenter's dark house.
And silent stood beneath the shot-window;
Unto his breast it reached, it was so low;
510 And he coughed softly, in a low half tone:
"What do you, honeycomb, sweet Alison?
My cinnamon, my fair bird, my sweetie,
Awake, O darling mine, and speak to me!
It's little thought you give me and my woe,
515 Who for your love do sweat where'er I go.
Yet it's no wonder that I faint and sweat;
I long as does the lamb for mother's teat.
Truly, sweetheart, I have such love-longing
That like a turtle-dove's my true yearning;
520 And I can eat no more than can a maid."

     "Go from the window, jack-a-napes," she said,
"For, s'help me God, it is not 'come kiss me.'
I love another, or to blame I'd be,
Better than you, by Jesus, Absalom!
525 Go on your way, or I'll stone you therefrom,
And let me sleep, the fiends take you away!"
     "Alas," quoth Absalom, "and welaway!
That true love ever was so ill beset!
But kiss me, since you'll do no more, my pet,
530 For Jesus' love and for the love of me."

     "And will you go, then, on your way?" asked she.
"Yes truly, darling," said this Absalom.
     "Then make you ready," said she, "and I'll come!"
And unto Nicholas said she, low and still:
535 "Be silent now, and you shall laugh your fill."
     This Absalom plumped down upon his knees,
And said: "I am a lord in all degrees;
For after this there may be better still!
Darling, my sweetest bird, I wait your will."
540   The window she unbarred, and that in haste.
"Have done," said she, "come on, and do it fast,
Before we're seen by any neighbour's eye."

This Absalom did wipe his mouth all dry;
Dark was the night as pitch, aye dark as coal,
545 And through the window she put out her hole.
And Absalom no better felt nor worse,
But with his mouth he kissed her naked arse
Right greedily, before he knew of this.
Aback he leapt—it seemed somehow amiss,
550 For well he knew a woman has no beard;
He'd felt a thing all rough and longish haired,
And said, "Oh fie, alas! What did I do?"
"Teehee!" she laughed, and clapped the window to;
And Absalom went forth a sorry pace.
555 "A beard! A beard! cried clever Nicholas,
"Now by God's *corpus,*[58] this goes fair and well!"   [58]*body*
This hapless Absalom, he heard that yell,
And on his lip, for anger, he did bite;
And to himself he said, "I will requite!"
560 Who vigorously rubbed and scrubbed his lips
With dust, with sand, with straw, with cloth, with chips,
But Absalom, and often cried "Alas!
My soul I give now unto Sathanas,
For rather far than own this town," said he,
565 "For this despite, it's well revenged I'd be.
Alas," said he, "from her I never blenched!"[59]   [59]*turned away*
His hot love was grown cold, aye and all quenched;
For, from the moment that he'd kissed her arse,
For paramours he didn't care a curse,
570 For he was healed of all his malady;
Indeed all paramours he did defy,
And wept as does a child that has been beat.
With silent step he went across the street
Unto a smith whom men called Sir Jarvis,
575 Who in his smithy forged plow parts, that is   [60]*plowshares*
He sharpened shares[60] and coulters[61] busily.
This Absalom he knocked all easily,   [61]*cutting blades of plows*
And said, "Unbar here, Jarvis, for I come."
"What! Who are you?"
580   "It's I, it's Absalom."   [62]*a Latin word used as a standard greeting of goodwill*
"What! Absalom! For Jesus Christ's sweet tree,
Why are you up so early? *Ben'cite!*[62]

What ails you now, man? Some gay girl, God knows,
Has brought you on the jump to my bellows;
By Saint Neot,[63] you know well what I mean."
585   This Absalom cared not a single bean
For all this play, nor one word back he gave;
He'd more tow on his distaff,[64] had this knave,
Than Jarvis knew, and said he: "Friend so dear,
This red-hot coulter in the fireplace here,
590 Lend it to me, I have a need for it,
And I'll return it after just a bit."
        Jarvis replied: "Certainly, were it gold
Or a purse filled with yellow coins untold,
Yet should you have it, as I am true smith;
595 But eh, Christ's foe! What will you do therewith?
        "Let that," said Absalom, "be as it may;
I'll tell you all tomorrow, when it's day"—
And caught the coulter then by the cold steel
And softly from the smithy door did steal
600 And went again up to the wood-wright's wall.
He coughed at first, and then he knocked withal
Upon the window, as before, with care.
        This Alison replied: "Now who is there?
And who knocks so? I'll warrant it's a thief."
605   "Why no," quoth he, "God knows, my sweet rose-leaf,
I am your Absalom, my own darling!
Of gold," quoth he, "I have brought you a ring;
My mother gave it me, as I'll be saved;
Fine gold it is, and it is well engraved;
610 This will I give you for another kiss."
        This Nicholas had risen for a piss,
And thought that it would carry on the jape
To have his arse kissed by this jack-a-nape.
And so he opened window hastily,
615 And put his arse out thereat, quietly,
Over the buttocks, showing the whole bum;
And thereto said this clerk, this Absalom,
"O speak, sweet bird, I know not where thou art."
This Nicholas just then let fly a fart
620 As loud as it had been a thunder-clap,
And well-nigh blinded Absalom, poor chap;

[63]a 9th-century
monk supposed
to have advised
the king to found
Oxford University

[64]flax on his spin-
ning staff (i.e.,
business to attend
to)

But he was ready with his iron hot
And Nicholas right in the arse he got.
　Off went the skin and hand's-breadth broad, about,
625　The coulter burned his bottom so, throughout,
That for the pain he thought that he should die.
And like one mad he started in to cry,
"Help! Water! Water! Help! For God's dear heart!"
　This carpenter out of his sleep did start,
630　Hearing that "Water!" cried as madman would,
And thought, "Alas, now comes down Noel's[65] flood!"
He struggled up without another word
And with his axe he cut in two the cord,
And down went all; he did not stop to trade
635　In bread or ale till he'd the journey made,
And there upon the floor he swooning lay.
　Up started Alison and Nicholay
And shouted "Help!" and "Hello!" down the street.
The neighbors, great and small, with hastening feet
640　Swarmed in the house to stare upon this man,
Who lay yet swooning, and all pale and wan;
For in the falling he had smashed his arm.
He had to suffer, too, another harm,
For when he spoke he was at once borne down
645　By clever Nicholas and Alison.
For they told everyone that he was odd;[66]
He was so much afraid of "Noel's" flood,
Through fantasy, that out of vanity
He'd gone and bought these kneading-tubs, all three,
650　And that he'd hung them near the roof above;
And that he had prayed them, for God's dear love,
To sit with him and bear him company.
　The people laughed at all this fantasy;
Up to the roof they looked, and there did gape,
655　And so turned all his injury to a jape.
For when this carpenter got in a word,
'Twas all in vain, no man his reasons heard;
With oaths impressive he was so sworn down
That he was held for mad by all the town;
660　For every clerk did side with every other.
They said: "The man is crazy, my dear brother."

[65]*Noah's*

[66]*crazy*

[67]*slept with*

And everyone did laugh at all this strife.
    Thus futtered[67] was the carpenter's goodwife,
For all his watching and his jealousy;
665 And Absalom has kissed her nether eye;
And Nicholas is branded on the butt.
This tale is done, and God save all the rout.[68]

[68]*crowd*

Wife *The* of Bath's

PROLOGUE

EXPERIENCE, though no authority
Were in this world, were good enough for me,
To speak of woe that is in all marriage;
For, masters, since I was twelve years of age,
5 Thanks be to God, Who is for aye alive,
Of husbands at church door have I had five;
For men so many times have wedded me;
And all were worthy men in their degree.
But someone told me not so long ago
10 That since Our Lord, save once, would never go
To wedding (that at Cana in Galilee),[1]
Thus, by this same example, showed He me
I never should have married more than once.
    Lo and behold! What sharp words, for the nonce,
15 Beside a well Lord Jesus, God and man,
Spoke in reproving the Samaritan:[2]
'For thou hast had five husbands,' thus said He,
'And he whom thou hast now to be with thee
Is not thine husband.' Thus He said that day,
20 But what He meant thereby I cannot say;
And I would ask now why that same fifth man
Was not husband to the Samaritan?

[1] the wedding at which Jesus turned water into wine

[2] a person of Samaria, the northern part of Israel

How many might she have, then, in marriage?
For I have never heard, in all my age,
Clear exposition of this number shown,
Though men may guess and argue up and down.
25 But well I know and say, and do not lie,
God bade us to increase and multiply;
That worthy text can I well understand.
And well I know He said, too, my husband
Should father leave, and mother, and cleave to me;
30 But no specific number mentioned He,
Whether of bigamy or octogamy;[3]
Why should men speak of it reproachfully?
Lo, there's the wise old king Sir Solomon;
I understand he had more wives than one;
35 And now would God it were permitted me
To be refreshed one half as oft as he!
Which gift of God he had for all his wives!
No man has such that in this world now lives.
God knows, this noble king, it strikes my wit,
40 The first night he had many a merry fit
With each of them, so much he was alive!
Praise be to God that I have wedded five!
Of whom I did pick out and choose the best
Both for their nether purse and for their chest
45 Different schools make divers perfect clerks,
Different methods learned in sundry works
Make the good workman perfect, certainly.
Of full five husbands tutoring am I.
Welcome the sixth whenever come he shall.
50 Forsooth, I'll not keep chaste for good and all;
When my good husband from the world is gone,
Some Christian man shall marry me anon;
For then, the apostle says that I am free
To wed, in God's name, where it pleases me.
55 He says that to be wedded is no sin;
Better to marry than to burn within.
What care I though folk speak reproachfully
Of wicked Lamech[4] and his bigamy?
I know well Abraham was holy man,
60 And Jacob,[5] too, as far as know I can;
And each of them had spouses more than two;

[3] having eight husbands or wives

[4] the first bigamist in the Bible

[5] Abraham and Jacob are two biblical patriarchs.

And many another holy man also.
Or can you say that you have ever heard
That God has ever by His express word
65 Marriage forbidden? Pray you, now, tell me.
Or where commanded He virginity?
I read as well as you no doubt have read
The apostle when he speaks of maidenhead;
He said, commandment of the Lord he'd none.
70 Men may advise a woman to be one,
But such advice is not commandment, no;
He left the thing to our own judgment so.
For had Lord God commanded maidenhood,
He'd have condemned all marriage as not good;
75 And certainly, if there were no seed sown,
Virginity- where then should it be grown?
Paul dared not to forbid us, at the least,
A thing whereof his Master'd no behest.[6]
The dart[7] is set up for virginity;
80 Catch it who can; who runs best let us see.
      "But this word is not meant for every wight,
But where God wills to give it, of His might.
I know well that the apostle was a maid;
Nevertheless, and though he wrote and said
85 He would that everyone were such as he,
All is not counsel to virginity;
And so to be a wife he gave me leave
Out of permission; there's no shame should grieve
In marrying me, if that my mate should die,
90 Without exception, too, of bigamy.
And though 'twere good no woman flesh to touch,
He meant, in his own bed or on his couch;
For peril 'tis fire and tow to assemble;
You know what this example may resemble.
95 This is the sum: he held virginity
Nearer perfection than marriage for frailty.
And frailty's all, I say, save he and she
Would lead their lives throughout in chastity.
      "I grant this well, I have no great envy
100 Though maidenhood's preferred to bigamy;
Let those who will be clean, body and ghost,
Of my condition I will make no boast.

[6]*which his Master did not command*

[7]*a dart given as a prize*

For well you know, a lord in his household,
He has not every vessel all of gold;
105 Some are of wood and serve well all their days.
God calls folk unto Him in sundry ways,
And each one has from God a proper gift,

Some this, some that, as pleases Him to shift.[8]
"Virginity is great perfection known,
110 And continence e'en with devotion shown.
But Christ, Who of perfection is the well,
Bade not each separate man he should go sell
All that he had and give it to the poor
And follow Him in such wise going before.
115 He spoke to those that would live perfectly;
And, masters, by your leave, such am not I.
I will devote the flower of all my age
To all the acts and harvests of marriage.
"Tell me also, to what purpose or end
120 The genitals were made, that I defend,
And for what benefit was man first wrought?
Trust you right well, they were not made for naught.
Explain who will and argue up and down
That they were made for passing out, as known,
125 Of urine, and our two belongings small
Were just to tell a female from a male,
And for no other cause- ah, say you no?
Experience knows well it is not so;
And, so the clerics be not with me wroth,
130 I say now that they have been made for both,
That is to say, for duty and for ease
In getting, when we do not God displease.
Why should men otherwise in their books set
That man shall pay unto his wife his debt?
135 Now wherewith should he ever make payment,
Except he used his blessed instrument?
Then on a creature were devised these things
For urination and engenderings.
"But I say not that every one is bound,
140 Who's fitted out and furnished as I've found,
To go and use it to beget an heir;
Then men would have for chastity no care.
Christ was a maid, and yet shaped like a man,

And many a saint, since this old world began,
145 Yet has lived ever in perfect chastity.
I bear no malice to virginity;
Let such be bread of purest white wheat-seed,
And let us wives be called but barley bread;
And yet with barley bread (if Mark you scan)[9]
150 Jesus Our Lord refreshed full many a man.
In such condition as God places us
I'll persevere, I'm not fastidious.
In wifehood I will use my instrument
As freely as my Maker has it sent.
155 If I be niggardly, God give me sorrow!
My husband he shall have it, eve and morrow,
When he's pleased to come forth and pay his debt.
I'll not delay, a husband I will get
Who shall be both my debtor and my thrall
160 And have his tribulations therewithal
Upon his flesh, the while I am his wife.
I have the power during all my life
Over his own good body, and not he.
For thus the apostle told it unto me;
165 And bade our husbands that they love us well.
And all this pleases me whereof I tell."
     Up rose the pardoner, and that anon.
"Now dame," said he, "by God and by Saint John,
You are a noble preacher in this case!
170 I was about to wed a wife, alas!
Why should I buy this on my flesh so dear?
No, I would rather wed no wife this year."
     "But wait," said she, "my tale is not begun;
Nay, you shall drink from out another tun[10]
175 Before I cease, and savour worse than ale.
And when I shall have told you all my tale
Of tribulation that is in marriage,
Whereof I've been an expert all my age,
That is to say, myself have been the whip,
180 Then may you choose whether you will go sip
Out of that very tun which I shall broach.
Beware of it ere you too near approach;
For I shall give examples more than ten.
Whoso will not be warned by other men

[9] *if you read the book of Mark*

[10] *cask (of ale)*

[11] *a Greek
mathematician,
astronomer, and
geographer*

[12] *a book by
Ptolemy*

185 By him shall other men corrected be,
       The self-same words has written Ptolemy;[11]
       Read in his Almagest[12] and find it there."
          "Lady, I pray you, if your will it were,"
       Spoke up this pardoner, "as you began,
190 Tell forth your tale, nor spare for any man,
       And teach us younger men of your technique."
          "Gladly," said she, "since it may please, not pique.
       But yet I pray of all this company
       That if I speak from my own phantasy,
195 They will not take amiss the things I say;
       For my intention's only but to play.
          "Now, sirs, now will I tell you forth my tale.
       And as I may drink ever wine and ale,
       I will tell truth of husbands that I've had,
200 For three of them were good and two were bad.
       The three were good men and were rich and old.
       Not easily could they the promise hold
       Whereby they had been bound to cherish me.
       You know well what I mean by that, pardie!
205 So help me God, I laugh now when I think
       How pitifully by night I made them swink;
       And by my faith I set by it no store.
       They'd given me their gold, and treasure more;
       I needed not do longer diligence
210 To win their love, or show them reverence.
       They all loved me so well, by God above,
       I never did set value on their love!
       A woman wise will strive continually
       To get herself loved, when she's not, you see.
215 But since I had them wholly in my hand,
       And since to me they'd given all their land,
       Why should I take heed, then, that I should please,
       Save it were for my profit or my ease?
       I set them so to work, that, by my fay,

[13] *Married couples
who lived a year
and a day without
arguing won a
side of bacon.*

[14] *crow*

220 Full many a night they sighed out 'Welaway!'
       The bacon was not brought them home, I trow,
       That some men have in Essex at Dunmowe.[13]
       I governed them so well, by my own law,
       That each of them was happy as a daw,[14]
225 And fain to bring me fine things from the fair.

And they were right glad when I spoke them fair;
For God knows that I nagged them mercilessly.
　　"Now hearken how I bore me properly,
All you wise wives that well can understand.

230　　"Thus shall you speak and wrongfully demand;
For half so brazenfacedly can no man
Swear to his lying as a woman can.
I say not this to wives who may be wise,
Except when they themselves do misadvise.

235　A wise wife, if she knows what's for her good,
Will swear the crow is mad, and in this mood
Call up for witness to it her own maid;
But hear me now, for this is what I said.
　　"'Sir Dotard, is it thus you stand today?

240　Why is my neighbour's wife so fine and gay?
She's honoured over all where'er she goes;
I sit at home, I have no decent clo'es.
What do you do there at my neighbour's house?
Is she so fair? Are you so amorous?

245　Why whisper to our maid? Benedicite!
Sir Lecher old, let your seductions be!
And if I have a gossip or a friend,
Innocently, you blame me like a fiend
If I but walk, for company, to his house!

250　You come home here as drunken as a mouse,
And preach there on your bench, a curse on you!
You tell me it's a great misfortune, too,
To wed a girl who costs more than she's worth;
And if she's rich and of a higher birth,

255　You say it's torment to abide her folly
And put up with her pride and melancholy.
And if she be right fair, you utter knave,
You say that every lecher will her have;
She may no while in chastity abide

260　That is assailed by all and on each side.
　　"'You say, some men desire us for our gold,
Some for our shape and some for fairness told:
And some, that she can either sing or dance,
And some, for courtesy and dalliance;

265　Some for her hands and for her arms so small;
Thus all goes to the devil in your tale.

You say men cannot keep a castle wall
That's long assailed on all sides, and by all.
   "'And if that she be foul, you say that she
270 Hankers for every man that she may see;
For like a spaniel will she leap on him
Until she finds a man to be victim;
And not a grey goose swims there in the lake
But finds a gander willing her to take.
275 You say, it is a hard thing to enfold
Her whom no man will in his own arms hold.
This say you, worthless, when you go to bed;
And that no wise man needs thus to be wed,
No, nor a man that hearkens unto Heaven.

280 With furious thunder-claps and fiery levin[15]
May your thin, withered, wrinkled neck be broke:
   "'You say that dripping eaves, and also smoke,
And wives contentious, will make men to flee
Out of their houses; ah, benedicite!
285 What ails such an old fellow so to chide?
   "'You say that all we wives our vices hide
Till we are married, then we show them well;
That is a scoundrel's proverb, let me tell!
   "'You say that oxen, asses, horses, hounds
290 Are tried out variously, and on good grounds;
Basins and bowls, before men will them buy,
And spoons and stools and all such goods you try.
And so with pots and clothes and all array;
But of their wives men get no trial, you say,
295 Till they are married, base old dotard you!
And then we show what evil we can do.
   "'You say also that it displeases me
Unless you praise and flatter my beauty,
And save you gaze always upon my face
300 And call me "lovely lady" every place;
And save you make a feast upon that day
When I was born, and give me garments gay;
And save due honour to my nurse is paid
As well as to my faithful chambermaid,
305 And to my father's folk and his allies-
Thus you go on, old barrel full of lies!
   "'And yet of our apprentice, young Jenkin,

For his crisp hair, showing like gold so fine,
Because he squires me walking up and down,
310 A false suspicion in your mind is sown;
I'd give him naught, though you were dead tomorrow.
  "'But tell me this, why do you hide, with sorrow,
The keys to your strong-box away from me?
It is my gold as well as yours, pardie.
315 Why would you make an idiot of your dame?
Now by Saint James, but you shall miss your aim,
You shall not be, although like mad you scold,
Master of both my body and my gold;
One you'll forgo in spite of both your eyes;
320 Why need you seek me out or set on spies?
I think you'd like to lock me in your chest!
You should say: "Dear wife, go where you like best,
Amuse yourself, I will believe no tales;
You're my wife Alis[16] true, and truth prevails."

[16]*Alisoun*

325 We love no man that guards us or gives charge
Of where we go, for we will be at large.
  "'Of all men the most blessed may he be,
That wise astrologer, Sir Ptolemy,
Who says this proverb in his Almagest:
330 "Of all men he's in wisdom the highest
That nothing cares who has the world in hand."
And by this proverb shall you understand:
Since you've enough, why do you reck or care
How merrily all other folks may fare?
335 For certainly, old dotard, by your leave,
You shall have cunt all right enough at eve.
He is too much a niggard who's so tight
That from his lantern he'll give none a light.
For he'll have never the less light, by gad;
340 Since you've enough, you need not be so sad.
  "'You say, also, that if we make us gay
With clothing, all in costliest array,
That it's a danger to our chastity;
And you must back the saying up, pardie!
345 Repeating these words in the apostle's name:
"In habits meet for chastity, not shame,
Your women shall be garmented," said he,
"And not with broidered[17] hair, or jewellery,

[17]*braided*

[18]fashion

[19]words written in
red ink that head
a text

[20]to wail like a cat

Or pearls, or gold, or costly gowns and chic;"[18]
350 After your text and after your rubric[19]
I will not follow more than would a gnat.
You said this, too, that I was like a cat;
For if one care to singe a cat's furred skin,
Then would the cat remain the house within;
355 And if the cat's coat be all sleek and gay,
She will not keep in house a half a day,
But out she'll go, ere dawn of any day,
To show her skin and caterwaul[20] and play.
This is to say, if I'm a little gay,
360 To show my rags I'll gad about all day.
        "'Sir Ancient Fool, what ails you with your spies?
Though you pray Argus, with his hundred eyes,
To be my body-guard and do his best,
Faith, he sha'n't hold me, save I am modest;
365 I could delude him easily- trust me!
        "'You said, also, that there are three things- three-
The which things are a trouble on this earth,
And that no man may ever endure the fourth:
O dear Sir Rogue, may Christ cut short your life!
370 Yet do you preach and say a hateful wife
Is to be reckoned one of these mischances.
Are there no other kinds of resemblances
That you may liken thus your parables to,
But must a hapless wife be made to do?
375   "'You liken woman's love to very Hell,
To desert land where waters do not well.
You liken it, also, unto wildfire;
The more it burns, the more it has desire
To consume everything that burned may be.
380 You say that just as worms destroy a tree,
Just so a wife destroys her own husband;
Men know this who are bound in marriage band.'
        "Masters, like this, as you must understand,
Did I my old men charge and censure, and
385 Claim that they said these things in drunkenness;
And all was false, but yet I took witness
Of Jenkin and of my dear niece also.
O Lord, the pain I gave them and the woe,
All guiltless, too, by God's grief exquisite!

390 For like a stallion could I neigh and bite.
    I could complain, though mine was all the guilt,
    Or else, full many a time, I'd lost the tilt.
    Whoso comes first to mill first gets meal ground;
    I whimpered first and so did them confound.
395 They were right glad to hasten to excuse
    Things they had never done, save in my ruse.
        "With wenches would I charge him, by this hand,
    When, for some illness, he could hardly stand.
    Yet tickled this the heart of him, for he
400 Deemed it was love produced such jealousy.
    I swore that all my walking out at night
    Was but to spy on girls he kept outright;
    And under cover of that I had much mirth.
    For all such wit is given us at birth;
405 Deceit, weeping, and spinning, does God give
    To women, naturally, the while they live.
    And thus of one thing I speak boastfully,
    I got the best of each one, finally,
    By trick, or force, or by some kind of thing,
410 As by continual growls or murmuring;
    Especially in bed had they mischance,
    There would I chide and give them no pleasance;
    I would no longer in the bed abide
    If I but felt his arm across my side,
415 Till he had paid his ransom unto me;
    Then would I let him do his nicety.
    And therefore to all men this tale I tell,
    Let gain who may, for everything's to sell.
    With empty hand men may no falcons lure;
420 For profit would I all his lust endure,
    And make for him a well-feigned appetite;
    Yet I in bacon never had delight;
    And that is why I used so much to chide.
    For if the pope were seated there beside
425 I'd not have spared them, no, at their own board.
    For by my truth, I paid them, word for word.
    So help me the True God Omnipotent,
    Though I right now should make my testament,
    I owe them not a word that was not quit.
430 I brought it so about, and by my wit,

That they must give it up, as for the best,
Or otherwise we'd never have had rest.
For though he glared and scowled like lion mad,
Yet failed he of the end he wished he had.

435   "Then would I say: 'Good dearie, see you keep
In mind how meek is Wilkin, our old sheep;
Come near, my spouse, come let me kiss your cheek!
You should be always patient, aye, and meek,
And have a sweetly scrupulous tenderness,

440 Since you so preach of old Job's patience, yes.
Suffer always, since you so well can preach;
And, save you do, be sure that we will teach
That it is well to leave a wife in peace.
One of us two must bow, to be at ease;

445 And since a man's more reasonable, they say,
Than woman is, you must have patience aye.
What ails you that you grumble thus and groan?
Is it because you'd have my queynte[21] alone?
Why take it all, lo, have it every bit;

450 Peter! Beshrew you but you're fond of it!
For if I would go peddle my belle chose,[22]
I could walk out as fresh as is a rose;
But I will keep it for your own sweet tooth.
You are to blame, by God I tell the truth.'

455   "Such were the words I had at my command.
Now will I tell you of my fourth husband.
    "My fourth husband, he was a reveller,
That is to say, he kept a paramour;
And young and full of passion then was I,

460 Stubborn and strong and jolly as a pie.
Well could I dance to tune of harp, nor fail
To sing as well as any nightingale
When I had drunk a good draught of sweet wine.
Metellius,[23] the foul churl and the swine,

465 Did with a staff deprive his wife of life
Because she drank wine; had I been his wife
He never should have frightened me from drink;
For after wine, of Venus must I think:
For just as surely as cold produces hail,

470 A liquorish mouth must have a lickerish[24] tail.
In women wine's no bar of impotence,

[21]*female genitalia*

[22]*body (used in a sexual sense)*

[23]*Egnatius Metellus*

[24]*lecherous*

This know all lechers by experience.

 "But Lord Christ! When I do remember me
Upon my youth and on my jollity,
475 It tickles me about my heart's deep root.
To this day does my heart sing in salute
That I have had my world in my own time.
But age, alas! that poisons every prime,
Has taken away my beauty and my pith;
480 Let go, farewell, the devil go therewith!
The flour is gone, there is no more to tell,
The bran, as best I may, must I now sell;
But yet to be right merry I'll try, and
Now will I tell you of my fourth husband.
485 "I say that in my heart I'd great despite
When he of any other had delight.
But he was quit by God and by Saint Joce![25]
I made, of the same wood, a staff most gross;
Not with my body and in manner foul,
490 But certainly I showed so gay a soul
That in his own thick grease I made him fry
For anger and for utter jealousy.
By God, on earth I was his purgatory,
For which I hope his soul lives now in glory.
495 For God knows, many a time he sat and sung
When the shoe bitterly his foot had wrung.
There was no one, save God and he, that knew
How, in so many ways, I'd twist the screw.
He died when I came from Jerusalem,
500 And lies entombed beneath the great rood-beam,
Although his tomb is not so glorious
As was the sepulchre of Darius,[26]
The which Apelles wrought full cleverly;
'Twas waste to bury him expensively.
505 Let him fare well. God give his soul good rest,
He now is in the grave and in his chest.

  "And now of my fifth husband will I tell.
God grant his soul may never get to Hell!
And yet he was to me most brutal, too;
510 My ribs yet feel as they were black and blue,
And ever shall, until my dying day.
But in our bed he was so fresh and gay,

[25] St. Judocus, a saint, who was identified with a wooden staff, whose relics were at the Hyde Abbey; the abbot of the Hyde Abbey also owned the Tabard Inn.

[26] a king of Persia

And therewithal he could so well impose,
What time he wanted use of my belle chose,
515 That though he'd beaten me on every bone,
He could re-win my love, and that full soon.
I guess I loved him best of all, for he
Gave of his love most sparingly to me.
We women have, if I am not to lie,
520 In this love matter, a quaint fantasy;
Look out a thing we may not lightly have,
And after that we'll cry all day and crave.
Forbid a thing, and that thing covet we;
Press hard upon us, then we turn and flee.
525 Sparingly offer we our goods, when fair;
Great crowds at market for dearer ware,
And what's too common brings but little price;
All this knows every woman who is wise.
      "My fifth husband, may God his spirit bless!
530 Whom I took all for love, and not riches,
Had been sometime a student at Oxford,
And had left school and had come home to board
With my best gossip, dwelling in our town,
God save her soul! Her name was Alison.
535 She knew my heart and all my privity
Better than did our parish priest, s'help me!
To her confided I my secrets all.
For had my husband pissed against a wall,
Or done a thing that might have cost his life,
540 To her and to another worthy wife,
And to my niece whom I loved always well,
I would have told it—every bit I'd tell,
And did so, many and many a time, God wot,
Which made his face full often red and hot
545 For utter shame; he blamed himself that he
Had told me of so deep a privity.
      "So it befell that on a time, in Lent
(For oftentimes I to my gossip went,
Since I loved always to be glad and gay
550 And to walk out, in March, April, and May,
From house to house, to hear the latest malice),
Jenkin the clerk, and my gossip Dame Alis,
And I myself into the meadows went.

My husband was in London all that Lent;
555 I had the greater leisure, then, to play,
And to observe, and to be seen, I say,
By pleasant folk; what knew I where my face
Was destined to be loved, or in what place?
Therefore I made my visits round about
560 To vigils and processions of devout,
To preaching too, and shrines of pilgrimage,
To miracle plays, and always to each marriage,
And wore my scarlet skirt before all wights.
These worms and all these moths and all these mites,
565 I say it at my peril, never ate;
And know you why? I wore it early and late.

   "Now will I tell you what befell to me.
I say that in the meadows walked we three
Till, truly, we had come to such dalliance,
570 This clerk and I, that, of my vigilance,
I spoke to him and told him how that he,
Were I a widow, might well marry me.
For certainly I say it not to brag,
But I was never quite without a bag
575 Full of the needs of marriage that I seek.
I hold a mouse's heart not worth a leek
That has but one hole into which to run,
And if it fail of that, then all is done.

   "I made him think he had enchanted me;
580 My mother taught me all that subtlety.
And then I said I'd dreamed of him all night,
He would have slain me as I lay upright,
And all my bed was full of very blood;
But yet I hoped that he would do me good,
585 For blood betokens gold, as I was taught.
And all was false, I dreamed of him just—naught,
Save as I acted on my mother's lore,
As well in this thing as in many more.

   "But now, let's see, what was I going to say?
590 Aha, by God, I know! It goes this way.

   "When my fourth husband lay upon his bier,
I wept enough and made but sorry cheer,
As wives must always, for it's custom's grace,
And with my kerchief covered up my face;

595 But since I was provided with a mate,
    I really wept but little, I may state.
        "To church my man was borne upon the morrow
    By neighbours, who for him made signs of sorrow;
    And Jenkin, our good clerk, was one of them.

27a mass given in honor of a dead person

600 So help me God, when rang the requiem[27]
    After the bier, I thought he had a pair
    Of legs and feet so clean-cut and so fair
    That all my heart I gave to him to hold.
    He was, I think, but twenty winters old,

605 And I was forty, if I tell the truth;
    But then I always had a young colt's tooth.
    Gap-toothed I was, and that became me well;
    I had the print of holy Venus' seal.
    So help me God, I was a healthy one,

28female genitalia

29feminine (ruled by Venus)

30masculine (ruled by Mars)

31born under the astrological sign of Taurus

32The planet Mars was in the constellation Taurus.

33Referring to the sign of Taurus, which Venus rules; all of these allusions to astrology point out that Alisoun was destined to be unchaste.

610 And fair and rich and young and full of fun;
    And truly, as my husbands all told me,
    I had the silkiest quoniam[28] that could be.
    For truly, I am all Venusian[29]
    In feeling, and my brain is Martian.[30]

615 Venus gave me my lust, my lickerishness,
    And Mars gave me my sturdy hardiness.
    Taurus was my ascendant,[31] with Mars[32] therein.
    Alas, alas, that ever love was sin!
    I followed always my own inclination

620 By virtue of my natal constellation;
    Which wrought me so I never could withdraw
    My Venus-chamber[33] from a good fellow.
    Yet have I Mars's mark upon my face,
    And also in another private place.

625 For God so truly my salvation be
    As I have never loved for policy,
    But ever followed my own appetite,
    Though he were short or tall, or black or white;
    I took no heed, so that he cared for me,

630 How poor he was, nor even of what degree.
        "What should I say now, save, at the month's end,
    This jolly, gentle, Jenkin clerk, my friend,
    Had wedded me full ceremoniously,
    And to him gave I all the land in fee

635 That ever had been given me before;

But, later I repented me full sore.
He never suffered me to have my way.
By God, he smote me on the ear, one day,
Because I tore out of his book a leaf,
640 So that from this my ear is grown quite deaf.
Stubborn I was as is a lioness,
And with my tongue a very jay,[34] I guess,
And walk I would, as I had done before,
From house to house, though I should not, he swore.
645 For which he oftentimes would sit and preach
And read old Roman tales to me and teach
How one Sulpicius Gallus left his wife
And her forsook for term of all his life
Because he saw her with bared head, I say,
650 Looking out from his door, upon a day.
    "Another Roman[35] told he of by name
Who, since his wife was at a summer-game
Without his knowing, he forsook her eke.
And then would he within his Bible seek
655 That proverb of the old Ecclesiast[36]
Where he commands so freely and so fast
That man forbid his wife to gad about;
Then would he thus repeat, with never doubt:
'Whoso would build his whole house out of sallows,
660 And spur his blind horse to run over fallows,
And let his wife alone go seeking hallows,
Is worthy to be hanged upon the gallows.'
But all for naught, I didn't care a haw
For all his proverbs, nor for his old saw,
665 Nor yet would I by him corrected be.
I hate one that my vices tells to me,
And so do more of us- God knows!- than I.
This made him mad with me, and furiously,
That I'd not yield to him in any case.
670   'Now will I tell you truth, by Saint Thomas[37]
Of why I tore from out his book a leaf
For which he struck me so it made me deaf.
    "He had a book that gladly, night and day
For his amusement he would read always.
675 Called 'Theophrastus' and 'Valeriou',[38]
At which book would he laugh uproarious

[39] *a monk who decreed that marriage was greater than chastity*

[40] *a theologian whose works opposed marriage*

[41] *mentioned by Jerome, but otherwise, an unknown reference*

[42] *a female author and doctor*

[43] *the lover and pupil of Abelard, mentioned in Ovid's Ars amatoria ("Ovid's Art")*

And, too, there sometime was a clerk at Rome,
A cardinal, that men called Saint Jerome,
Who made a book against Jovinian;[39]
680 In which book, too, there was Tertullian,[40]
Chrysippus,[41] Trotula,[42] and Heloise[43]
Who was abbess near Paris' diocese;
And too, the Proverbs of King Solomon,
And Ovid's Art, and books full many a one.
685 And all of these were bound in one volume.
And every night and day 'twas his custom,
When he had leisure and took some vacation
From all his other worldly occupation,
To read, within this book, of wicked wives.
690 He knew of them more legends and more lives
Than are of good wives written in the Bible.
For trust me well, it is impossible
That any cleric shall speak well of wives,
Unless it be of saints and holy lives,
695 But naught for other women will they do.
Who painted first the lion, tell me who?
By God, if women had but written stories,
As have these clerks within their oratories,
They would have written of men more wickedness
700 Than all the race of Adam could redress.
The children of Mercury and of Venus
Are in their lives antagonistic thus;
For Mercury loves wisdom and science,
And Venus loves but pleasure and expense.
705 Because they different dispositions own,
Each falls when other's in ascendant shown.
And God knows Mercury is desolate
In Pisces, wherein Venus rules in state;
And Venus falls when Mercury is raised;
710 Therefore no woman by a clerk is praised.
A clerk, when he is old and can naught do
Of Venus' labours worth his worn-out shoe,
Then sits he down and writes, in his dotage,[44]
That women cannot keep vow of marriage!
715   "But now to tell you, as I started to,
Why I was beaten for a book, pardieu.
Upon a night Jenkin, who was our sire,[45]

[44] *senility*

[45] *lord of the house*

Read in his book, as he sat by the fire,
Of Mother Eve who, by her wickedness,
720 First brought mankind to all his wretchedness
For which Lord Jesus Christ Himself was slain,
Who, with His heart's blood, saved us thus again.
Lo, here plainly of woman may you find
That woman was the ruin of mankind.
725 Then read he out how Samson[46] lost his hairs
When sleeping, his mistress cut them with her shears;
And through this treason lost he either eye.
"Then read he out, if I am not to lie,
Of Hercules, and Deianira's desire
730 That caused him to go set himself on fire.
And nothing escaped him of the pain and woe
That Socrates[47] had with his spouses two;"
How Xantippe[48] threw piss upon his head;
This hapless man sat still, as he were dead;
735 He wiped his head, no more durst he complain
Than 'Ere the thunder ceases comes the rain.'
"Then of Pasiphae,[49] the queen of Crete,
For cursedness he thought the story sweet;
Fie! Say no more—it is an awful thing—
740 Of her so horrible lust and love-liking.
"Of Clytemnestra,[50] for her lechery,
Who caused her husband's death by treachery,
He read all thus with greatest zest, I vow.
    "He told me, too, just when it was and how
745 Amphiaraus[51] at Thebes lost his life;
My husband had a legend of his wife
Eriphyle[52] who, for a brooch of gold,
In secrecy to hostile Greeks had told
Whereat her husband had his hiding place,
750 For which he found at Thebes but sorry grace.
"Of Livia[53] and Lucia[54] told he me,
For both of them their husbands killed, you see,
The one for love, the other killed for hate;
Livia her husband, on an evening late,
755 Made drink some poison, for she was his foe.
Lucia, lecherous, loved her husband so
That, to the end he'd always of her think,
She gave him such a, philtre,[55] for love-drink,

[46] in the Bible, a hero betrayed by his mistress

[47] a Greek philosopher; supposed to have an irritable wife

[48] the wife of Socrates

[49] the wife of Minos and who Poseidon cursed to procreate with a bull, thus, creating the Minotaur

[50] killed her husband, Agamemnon

[51] man who died at Thebes after following his wife's advice

[52] the wife of Amphiaraus

[53] a Roman woman said to have murdered her husband

[54] a Roman woman who poisoned her husband by mistake

[55] potion

That he was dead or ever it was morrow;
760 And husbands thus, by same means, came to sorrow.
Then did he tell how one Latumius
Complained unto his comrade Arrius
That in his garden grew a baleful tree
Whereon, he said, his wives, and they were three,
765 Had hanged themselves for wretchedness and woe.
'Dear brother,' Arrius said, 'and did they so?
Give me a graft of that same blessed tree
And in my garden planted it shall be!'
Of wives of later date he also read,
770 How some had slain their husbands in their bed
And let their lovers shag them all the night
While corpses lay upon the floor upright.
And some had driven nails into the brain
While husbands slept and in such wise were slain.
775 And some had given them poison in their drink.
He told more evil than the mind can think.
And therewithal he knew of more proverbs
Than in this world there grows of grass or herbs.
'Better,' he said, 'your habitation be
780 With lion wild or dragon foul,' said he,
'Than with a woman who will nag and chide.'
'Better,' he said, 'on the housetop abide
Than with a brawling wife down in the house;
Such are so wicked and contrarious
785 They hate the thing their husband loves, for aye.'
And when I saw he'd never make an end
Of reading in this cursed book at night,
Three leaves of it I snatched and tore outright
Out of his book, right as he read; also
790 Upon the cheek I gave him such a blow
That in our fire he reeled and fell right down.
Then he got up as does a wild lion,
And with his fist he struck me on the head,
And on the floor I lay as I were dead.
795 And when he saw how limp and still I lay,
He was afraid and would have run away,
Until at last out of my swoon I made:
'Oh, have you slain me, you false thief?' I said,

'And for my land have you thus murdered me?
800   Kiss me before I die, and let me be.'"
      "He came to me and near me he knelt down,
      And said: 'O my dear sister Alison,
      So help me God, I'll never strike you more;
      What I have done, you are to blame therefor.
805   But all the same, forgiveness now I seek!'
      And thereupon I hit him on the cheek,
      And said: 'Thief, so much vengeance do I wreak
      Now will I die, I can no longer speak!'
      But at the last, and with much care and woe,
810   We made it up between ourselves. And so
      He put the bridle reins within my hand
      To have the governing of house and land;
      And of his tongue and of his hand, also;
      And I made him burn his book, right then, oho!
815   And when I had thus gathered unto me
      By mastery all sovereignty,
      And he had said: 'My own true wedded wife,
      Do as you please the term of all your life;
      Keep your honor, and also my estate'—
820   After that day we never had debate.
      God help me so, I was to him as kind
      As any wife from Denmark unto Inde,
      And also true, and so was he to me.
      I pray to God, that sits in majesty,
825   So bless his soul for all his mercy dear.
      Now will I say my tale, if you will hear."

Wife of Bath

NOW IN THE OLDEN days of King Arthur,[1]
Of whom the Britons speak with great honour,
All this wide land was land of faery.
The elf-queen, with her jolly company,
5　Danced oftentimes on many a green mead;[2]
This was the old opinion, as I read.
I speak of many hundred years ago;
But now no man can see the elves, you know.
For now the so-great charity and prayers
10　Of limiters and other holy friars
That do infest each land and every stream
As thick as motes are in a bright sunbeam,
Blessing halls, chambers, kitchens, ladies' bowers,
Cities and towns and castles and high towers,
15　Villages, barns, cowsheds and dairies—
This causes it that there are now no fairies.
For where was wont to walk full many an elf,
Right there walks now the limiter himself
In both the later and early mornings,
20　Saying his matins[3] and such holy things,
As he goes round his district in his gown.
Women may now go safely up and down,

[1] *a legendary British king*

[2] *meadow*

[3] *morning prayers*

137

In every copse or under every tree;
There is no other incubus[4] than he,
25 And would do them naught but dishonour.
    And so befell it that this King Arthur
    Had at his court a lusty bachelor
    Who, on a day, came riding from river;
    And happened that, alone as she was born,
30 He saw a maiden walking through the corn,
    From whom, in spite of all she did and said,
    Straightway by force he took her maidenhead;
    For which violation was there such clamour,
    And such appealing unto King Arthur,
35 That soon condemned was this knight to be dead
    By course of law, and should have lost his head,
    Peradventure, such being the statute then;
    But that the other ladies and the queen
    So long prayed of the king to show him grace,
40 He granted life, at last, in the law's place,
    And gave him to the queen, as she should will,
    Whether she'd save him, or his blood should spill.
        The queen she thanked the king with all her might,
    And after this, thus spoke she to the knight,
45 When she'd an opportunity, one day:
    "You stand yet," said she, "in such poor a way
    That for your life you've no security.
    I'll grant you life if you can tell to me
    What thing it is that women most desire.
50 Be wise, and keep your neck from iron dire!
    And if you cannot tell it me anon,
    Then will I give you license to be gone
    A twelvemonth and a day, to search and learn
    Sufficient answer in this grave concern.
55 And your knight's word I'll have, ere forth you pace,
    To yield your body to me in this place."
    Grieved was this knight, and sorrowfully he sighed;
    But there! he could not do as pleased his pride.
    And at the last he chose that he would wend
60 And come again upon the twelvemonth's end,
    With such an answer as God might purvey;
    And so he took his leave and went his way.
    He sought out every house and every place

[4] an evil spirit which preyed on women sexually

Wherein he hoped to find that he had grace
65 To learn what women love the most of all;
But nowhere ever did it him befall
To find, upon the question stated here,
Two persons who agreed with statement clear.
  Some said that women all loved best riches,
70 Some said, fair fame, and some said, prettiness;
Some, rich array, some said 'twas lust abed
And often to be widowed and re-wed.
  Some said that our poor hearts are aye most eased
When we have been most flattered and thus pleased.
75 And he went near the truth, I will not lie;
A man may win us best with flattery;
And with attentions and with busyness
We're often limed,[5] the greater and the less.
And some say, too, that we do love the best
80 To be quite free to do our own behest,
And that no man reprove us for our vice,
But saying we are wise, take our advice.
For truly there is no one of us all,
If anyone shall rub us on a gall,
85 That will not kick because he tells the truth.
Try, and he'll find, who does so, I say sooth.
No matter how much vice we have within,
We would be held for wise and clean of sin.
To be held constant, also trustworthy,
90 And on one purpose steadfastly to dwell,
And not betray a thing that men may tell.
But that tale is not worth a rake's handle,
For God knows, we women can no thing conceal.
As witness Midas. Would you hear the tale?
95   Ovid, among some other matters small,
Said Midas had beneath his long curled hair,
Two ass's ears that grew in secret there,
The which defect he hid, as best he might,
Full cunningly from every person's sight,
100 And, save his wife, no one knew of it, no.
He loved her most, and trusted her also;
And he prayed of her that to no creature
She'd tell of his disfigurement impure.
  She swore him: Nay, for all this world to win

[5]*caught*

105 She would do no such villainy or sin
  And cause her husband have so foul a name;
  Nor would she tell it for her own deep shame.
  Nevertheless, she thought she would have died
  Because so long the secret must she hide;
110 It seemed to swell so big about her heart
  That some word from her mouth must surely start;
  And since she dared to tell it to no man,
  Down to a marsh, that lay hard by, she ran;
  Till she came there her heart was all afire,
115 And as a bittern[6] booms in the quagmire,
  She laid her mouth low to the water down:
  "Betray me not, you sounding water blown,"
  Said she, "I tell it to none else but you:
  Long ears like asses' has my husband two!
120 Now is my heart at ease, since that is out;
  I could no longer keep it, there's no doubt."
  Here may you see, though for a while we bide,
  Yet out it must; no secret can we hide.
  The rest of all this tale, if you would hear,
125 Read Ovid: in his book does it appear.
    This knight my tale is chiefly told about
  When what the knight went for he could not find out,
  That is, the thing that women love the best,
  Most saddened was the spirit in his breast;
130 But home he goes, he could no more delay.
  The day was come when home he turned his way;
  And on his way it chanced that he should ride
  In all his care, beneath a forest's side,
  And there he saw, a-dancing him before,
135 Full four and twenty ladies, maybe more;
  Toward which dance eagerly did he turn
  In hope that there some wisdom he should learn.
  But truly, ere he came upon them there,
  The dancers vanished all, he knew not where.
140 No creature saw he that gave sign of life,
  Save, on the greensward sitting, an old wife;
  A fouler person could no man devise.
  Before the knight this old wife did arise,
  And said: "Sir knight, hence lies no travelled way.
145 Tell me what thing you seek, and by your fay,[7]

[6]heron

[7]faith

Perchance you'll find it may the better be;
These ancient folk know many things," said she.
    "Dear mother," said this knight assuredly
"I am but dead, save I can tell, truly,
150 What thing it is that women most desire;
Could you inform me, I'd pay well your hire."
      "Plight[8] me your troth[9] here, hand in hand," said she,
"That you will do, whatever it may be,
The thing I ask if it lie in your might;
155 And I'll give you your answer ere the night."
      "Have here my word," said he. "That thing I grant."
"Then," said the crone, "of this I make my vaunt,
Your life is safe; and I will stand thereby,
Upon my life, the queen will say as I.
160 Let's see which is the proudest of them all
That wears upon her hair kerchief or caul,[10]
Shall dare say no to that which I shall teach;
Let us go now and without longer speech."
      Then whispered she a sentence in his ear,
165 And bade him to be glad and have no fear.
When they were come unto the court, this knight
Said he had kept his promise as was right,
And ready was his answer, as he said.
Full many a noble wife, and many a maid,
170 And many a widow, since they are so wise,
The queen herself sitting as high justice,
Assembled were, his answer there to hear;
And then the knight was bidden to appear.
      Command was given for silence in the hall,
175 And that the knight should tell before them all
What thing all worldly women love the best.
This knight did not stand dumb, as does a beast,
But to this question presently answered
With manly voice, so that the whole court heard:
180   "My liege[11] lady, generally," said he,
"Women desire to have the sovereignty
As well upon their husband as their love,
And to have mastery their man above;
This thing you most desire, though me you kill
185 Do as you please, I am here at your will."
      In all the court there was no wife or maid

[8]*pledge*

[9]*vow*

[10]*hairnet*

[11]*superior*

Or widow that denied the thing he said,
But all held, he was worthy to have life.
    And with that word up started the old wife
190 Whom he had seen a-sitting on the green.
"Mercy," cried she, "my sovereign lady queen!
Before the court's dismissed, give me my right.
'Twas I who taught the answer to this knight;
For which he did plight troth to me, out there,
195 That the first thing I should of him require
He would do that, if it lay in his might.
Before the court, now, pray I you, sir knight,"
Said she, "that you will take me for your wife;
For well you know that I have saved your life.
200 If this be false, say nay, upon your fay!"
    This knight replied: "Alas and welaway!
That I so promised I will not protest.
But for God's love pray make a new request,
Take all my wealth and let my body go."
205   "Nay then," said she, "beshrew us if I do!
For though I may be foul and old and poor,
I will not, for all metal and all ore
That from the earth is dug or lies above,
Be aught except your wife and your true love."
210   "My love?" cried he, "nay, rather my damnation!
Alas! that any of my race and station
Should ever so dishonoured foully be!"
    But all for naught; the end was this, that he
Was so constrained he needs must go and wed,
215 And take his ancient wife and go to bed.
Now, peradventure, would some men say here,
That, of my negligence, I take no care
To tell you of the joy and all the array
That at the wedding feast were seen that day.
220 Make a brief answer to this thing I shall;
I say, there was no joy or feast at all;
There was but heaviness and grievous sorrow;
For privately he wedded on the morrow,
And all day, then, he hid him like an owl;
225 So sad he was, his old wife looked so foul.
    Great was the woe the knight had in his thought
When he, with her, to marriage bed was brought;

He rolled about and turned him to and fro.
His old wife lay there, always smiling so,
230 And said: "O my dear husband, ben'cite!
Fares every knight with wife as you with me?
Is this the custom in King Arthur's house?
Are knights of his all so fastidious?
I am your own true love and, more, your wife;
235 And I am she who saved your very life;
And truly, since I've never done you wrong,
Why do you treat me so, this first night long?
You act as does a man who's lost his wit;
What is my fault? For God's love tell me it,
240 And it shall be amended, if I may."
    "Amended!" cried this knight, "Alas, nay, nay!
It will not be amended ever, no!
You are so loathsome, and so old also,
And therewith of so low a race were born,
245 It's little wonder that I toss and turn.
Would God my heart would break within my breast!"
    "Is this," asked she, "the cause of your unrest?"
"Yes, truly," said he, "and no wonder 'tis."
    "Now, sir," said she, "I could amend all this,
250 If I but would, and that within days three,
If you would bear yourself well towards me.
But since you speak of such gentility
As is descended from old wealth, till ye
Claim that for that you should be gentlemen,
255 I hold such arrogance not worth a hen.
Find him who is most virtuous alway,
Alone or publicly, and most tries aye
To do whatever noble deeds he can,
And take him for the greatest gentleman.
260 Christ wills we claim of Him our nobleness,
Not of our elders, for their old riches.
For though they give us all their heritage,
For which we claim to be of high lineage,
Yet can they not bequeath, in anything,
265 To any of us, their virtuous living,
That made men say they had gentility,
And bade us follow them in like degree.
    "Well does that poet wise of great Florence,

Called Dante,[12] speak his mind in this sentence;
270 Somewhat like this may it translated be:
'Rarely unto the branches of the tree
Doth human worth mount up: and so ordains
He Who bestows it; to Him it pertains.'
For of our fathers may we nothing claim
275 But temporal things, that man may hurt and maim
"And everyone knows this as well as I,
If nobleness were implanted naturally
Within a certain lineage, down the line,
In private and in public, I opine,
280 The ways of gentleness they'd always show
And never fall to vice and conduct low.
"Take fire and carry it in the darkest house
Between here and the Mount of Caucasus,
And let men shut the doors and from them turn;
285 Yet will the fire as fairly blaze and burn
As twenty thousand men did it behold;
Its nature and its office it will hold,
On peril of my life, until it die.
"From this you see that true gentility
290 Is not allied to wealth a man may own,
Since folk do not their deeds, as may be shown,
As does the fire, according to its kind.
For God knows that men may full often find
A lord's son doing shame and villainy;
295 And he that prizes his gentility
In being born of some old noble house,
With ancestors both noble and virtuous,
But will himself do naught of noble deeds
Nor follow him to whose name he succeeds,
300 He is not gentle, be he duke or earl;
For acting churlish makes a man a churl.
Gentility is not just the renown
Of ancestors who have some greatness shown,
In which you have no portion of your own.
305 Your own gentility comes from God alone;
Thence comes our true nobility by grace,
It was not willed us with our rank and place
"Think how noble, as says Valerius,[13]
Was that same Tullius Hostilius,[14]

310 Who out of poverty rose to high estate.
Seneca and Boethius[15] inculcate,
Expressly (and no doubt it thus proceeds),
That he is noble who does noble deeds;
And therefore, husband dear, I thus conclude:

315 Although my ancestors mayhap were rude,
Yet may the High Lord God, and so hope I,
Grant me the grace to live right virtuously.
Then I'll be gentle when I do begin
To live in virtue and to do no sin.

320   "And when you me reproach for poverty,
The High God, in Whom we believe, say I,
In voluntary poverty lived His life.
And surely every man, or maid, or wife
May understand that Jesus, Heaven's King,

325 Would not have chosen vileness of living.
Glad poverty's an honest thing, that's plain,
Which Seneca[16] and other clerks maintain.
Whoso will be content with poverty,
I hold him rich, though not a shirt has he.

330 And he that covets much is a poor wight,
For he would gain what's all beyond his might.
But he that has not, nor desires to have,
Is rich, although you hold him but a knave."
    "True poverty, it sings right naturally;

335 Juvenal[17] gaily says of poverty:
'The poor man, when he walks along the way,
Before the robbers he may sing and play.'
Poverty's odious good, and, as I guess,
It is a stimulant to busyness;

340 A great improver, too, of sapience
In him that takes it all with due patience.
Poverty's this, though it seem misery-
Its quality may none dispute, say I.
Poverty often, when a man is low,

345 Makes him his God and even himself to know.
And poverty's an eye-glass, seems to me,
Through which a man his loyal friends may see.
Since you've received no injury from me,
Then why reproach me for my poverty.

350   "Now, sir, with age you have upbraided me;

[15] a Roman philosopher and writer

[16] a Roman author admired for his views on morality and upright living

[17] another Roman poet

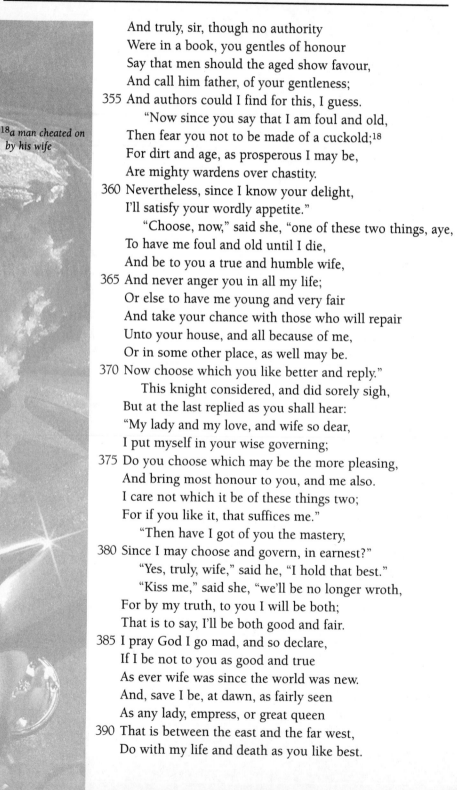

And truly, sir, though no authority
Were in a book, you gentles of honour
Say that men should the aged show favour,
And call him father, of your gentleness;
355 And authors could I find for this, I guess.
    "Now since you say that I am foul and old,
Then fear you not to be made of a cuckold;[18]
For dirt and age, as prosperous I may be,
Are mighty wardens over chastity.
360 Nevertheless, since I know your delight,
I'll satisfy your wordly appetite."
    "Choose, now," said she, "one of these two things, aye,
To have me foul and old until I die,
And be to you a true and humble wife,
365 And never anger you in all my life;
Or else to have me young and very fair
And take your chance with those who will repair
Unto your house, and all because of me,
Or in some other place, as well may be.
370 Now choose which you like better and reply."
    This knight considered, and did sorely sigh,
But at the last replied as you shall hear:
"My lady and my love, and wife so dear,
I put myself in your wise governing;
375 Do you choose which may be the more pleasing,
And bring most honour to you, and me also.
I care not which it be of these things two;
For if you like it, that suffices me."
    "Then have I got of you the mastery,
380 Since I may choose and govern, in earnest?"
    "Yes, truly, wife," said he, "I hold that best."
    "Kiss me," said she, "we'll be no longer wroth,
For by my truth, to you I will be both;
That is to say, I'll be both good and fair.
385 I pray God I go mad, and so declare,
If I be not to you as good and true
As ever wife was since the world was new.
And, save I be, at dawn, as fairly seen
As any lady, empress, or great queen
390 That is between the east and the far west,
Do with my life and death as you like best.

[18] *a man cheated on by his wife*

Throw back the curtain and see how it is."
    And when the knight saw verily all this,
That she so very fair was, and young too,
395 For joy he clasped her in his strong arms two,
His heart bathed in a bath of utter bliss;
A thousand times, all in a row, he'd kiss.
And she obeyed his wish in everything
This might give pleasure to his love-liking.
400   And thus they lived unto their lives' fair end,
In perfect joy; and Jesus to us send
Meek husbands, and young ones, fresh in bed,
And good luck to outlive them that we wed.
And I pray Jesus to cut short the lives
405 Of those who'll not be governed by their wives;
And old and querulous[19] niggards[20] with their pence,
And send them soon a mortal pestilence!

[19]*irritable*

[20]*misers*

The Pardoner's

P R O L O G U E

"MASTERS," QUOTH HE, "in churches, when I preach,
I am at pains that all shall hear my speech,
And ring it out as roundly as a bell,
For I know all by heart the thing I tell.
5 My theme is always one, and ever was:
'Radix malorum est cupiditas.'[1]
"First I announce the place whence I have come,
And then I show my pardons, all and some.
Our liege-lord's seal on my patent perfect,
10 I show that first, my safety to protect,
And then no man's so bold, no priest nor clerk,
As to disturb me in Christ's holy work;
And after that my tales I marshal all.
Indulgences of pope and cardinal,
15 Of patriarch and bishop, these I do
Show, and in Latin speak some words, a few,
To spice therewith a bit my sermoning
And stir men to devotion, marvelling.
Then show I forth my hollow crystal-stones,
20 Which are crammed full of rags, aye, and of bones;
Relics are these, as they think, every one.
Then I've in latten[2] box a shoulder bone
Which came out of a holy Hebrew's sheep.

[1] *Greed is the root of all evils (I Timothy: 6.10).*

[2] *thin brass*

149

'Good men,' say I, 'my words in memory keep;
25 If this bone shall be washed in any well,
Then if a cow, calf, sheep, or ox should swell
That's eaten snake, or been by serpent stung,
Take water of that well and wash its tongue,
And 'twill be well anon; and furthermore,
30 Of pox and scab and every other sore
Shall every sheep be healed that of this well
Drinks but one draught; take heed of what I tell.
And if the man that owns the beasts, I trow,
Shall every week, and that before cock-crow,
35 And before breakfast, drink thereof a draught,
As that Jew taught of yore in his priestcraft,
His beasts and all his store shall multiply.
And, good sirs, it's a cure for jealousy;
For though a man be fallen in jealous rage,
40 Let one make of this water his pottage³
And nevermore shall he his wife mistrust,
Though he may know the truth of all her lust,
Even though she'd taken two priests, aye, or three.
'"Here is a mitten, too, that you may see.
45 Who puts his hand therein, I say again,
He shall have increased harvest of his grain,
After he's sown, be it of wheat or oats,
Just so he offers pence⁴ or offers groats.⁵
'"Good men and women, one thing I warn you.
50 If any man be here in church right now
That's done a sin so horrible that he
Dare not, for shame, of that sin shriven be,
Or any woman, be she young or old,
That's made her husband into a cuckold,
55 Such folk shall have no power and no grace
To offer to my relics in this place.
But whoso finds himself without such blame,
He will come up and offer, in God's name,
And I'll absolve him by authority
60 That has, by bull, been granted unto me.'
"By this fraud have I won me, year by year,
A hundred marks, since I've been pardoner.
I stand up like a scholar in pulpit,
And when the ignorant people all do sit,

³soup
⁴pennies
⁵silver coins worth four pence

65 I preach, as you have heard me say before,
And tell a hundred false japes, less or more.
I am at pains, then, to stretch forth my neck,
And east and west upon the folk I beck,
As does a dove that's sitting on a barn.
70 With hands and swift tongue, then, do I so yarn
That it's a joy to see my busyness.
Of avarice and of all such wickedness
Is all my preaching, thus to make them free
With offered pence, the which pence come to me.
75 For my intent is only pence to win,
And not at all for punishment of sin.
When they are dead, for all I think thereon
Their souls may well black-berrying have gone!
For, certainly, there's many a sermon grows
80 Ofttimes from evil purpose, as one knows;
Some for folks' pleasure and for flattery,
To be advanced by all hypocrisy,
And some for vainglory, and some for hate.
For, when I dare not otherwise debate,
85 Then do I sharpen well my tongue and sting
The man in sermons, and upon him fling
My lying defamations, if but he
Has wronged my brethren or—much worse—wronged me.
For though I mention not his proper name,
90 Men know whom I refer to, all the same,
By signs I make and other circumstances.
Thus I pay those who do us displeasances.⁶
Thus spit I out my venom under hue
Of holiness, to seem both good and true.
95 "But briefly my intention I'll express;
I preach no sermon, save for covetousness.
For at my theme is yet, and ever was,
'Radix malorum est cupiditas.'
Thus can I preach against that self-same vice
100 Which I indulge, and that is avarice.
But though myself be guilty of that sin,
Yet can I cause these other folk to win
From avarice and really to repent.
But that is not my principal intent.
105 I preach no sermon, save for covetousness;

⁶*who displeases us*

This should suffice of that, though, as I guess.
"Then do I cite examples, many a one,
Out of old stories and of time long gone,
For vulgar people all love stories old;
110 Such things they can re-tell well and can hold.
What? Think you that because I'm good at preaching
And win me gold and silver by my teaching
I'll live of my free will in poverty?
No, no, that's never been my policy!
115 For I will preach and beg in sundry lands;
I will not work and labour with my hands,
Nor baskets weave and try to live thereby,
Because I will not beg in vain, say I.
I will none of the apostles counterfeit;
120 I will have money, wool, and cheese, and wheat,
Though it be given by the poorest page,
Or by the poorest widow in village,
And though her children perish of famine.
Nay! I will drink good liquor of the vine
125 And have a pretty wench in every town.
But hearken, masters, to conclusion shown:
Your wish is that I tell you all a tale.
Now that I've drunk a draught of musty ale,
By God, I hope that I can tell something
130 That shall, in reason, be to your liking.
For though I am myself a vicious man,
Yet I would tell a moral tale, and can,
The which I'm wont to preach more gold to win.
Now hold your peace! my tale I will begin."

The
Pardoner's
T A L E

IN FLANDERS, once, there was a company
Of young companions given to folly,
Riot and gambling, brothels and taverns;
And, to the music of harps, lutes, gitterns,[1]

¹*guitars*

5 They danced and played at dice both day and night,
And ate also and drank beyond their might,
Whereby they made the devil's sacrifice
Within that devil's temple, wicked wise,
By superfluity both vile and vain.
10 So damnable their oaths and so profane
That it was terrible to hear them swear;
Our blessed Saviour's Body did they tear;
They thought the Jews[2] had rent Him not enough;
And each of them at others' sins would laugh.

²*Jews had been*
expelled from
England in 1290,
but were still
a major source
of fascination
for English
Christians.

15 Then entered dancing-girls of ill repute,
Graceful and slim, and girls who peddled fruit,
Harpers and bawds[3] and women selling cake,
Who do their office for the Devil's sake,
To kindle and blow the fire of lechery,
20 Which is so closely joined with gluttony;
I call on holy writ, now, to witness
That lust is in all wine and drunkenness.

³*loose women*

Lo, how the drunken Lot unnaturally
Lay with his daughters two, unwittingly;
25 So drunk he was he knew not what he wrought.
Herod,[4] as in his story's clearly taught,
When full of wine and merry at a feast,
Sitting at table idly gave behest
To slay John Baptist, who was all guiltless.
30 Seneca says a good word too, doubtless;
He says there is no difference he can find
Between a man that's quite out of his mind
And one that's drunken, save perhaps in this
That when a wretch in madness fallen is,
35 The state lasts longer than does drunkenness.
O gluttony; full of all wickedness,
O first cause of confusion to us all,
Beginning of damnation and our fall,
Till Christ redeemed us with His blood again!
40 Behold how dearly, to be brief and plain,
Was purchased this accursed villainy;
Corrupt was all this world with gluttony!
Adam our father, and his wife also,
From Paradise to labour and to woe
45 Were driven for that vice, no doubt; indeed
The while that Adam fasted, as I read,
He was in Paradise; but then when he
Ate of the fruit forbidden of the tree,
Anon he was cast out to woe and pain.
50 O gluttony, of you we may complain!
Oh, knew a man how many maladies
Follow on excess and on gluttonies,
Surely he would be then more moderate
In diet, and at table more sedate.
55 Alas! The throat so short, the tender mouth,
Causing that east and west and north and south,
In earth, in air, in water men shall swink
To get a glutton dainty meat and drink!
Of this same matter Paul does wisely treat:
60 "Meat for the belly and belly for the meat:
And both shall God destroy," as Paul does say.
Alas! A foul thing is it, by my fay,
To speak this word, and fouler is the deed,

[4]the biblical king
who tried to kill
Jesus by order-
ing that all
male infants in
Bethlehem be
killed; in Piers
Plowman, Herod
is depicted as a
drunkard.

When man so guzzles of the white and red

65 That of his own throat makes he his privy,
Because of this cursed superfluity.
The apostle, weeping, says most piteously:
"For many walk, of whom I've told you, aye,
Weeping I tell you once again they're dross,

70 For they are foes of Christ and of the Cross,
Whose end is death, whose belly is their god."
O gut! O belly! O you stinking cod,
Filled full of dung, with all corruption found!
At either end of you foul is the sound.

75 With how great cost and labour do they find
Your food! These cooks, they pound and strain and grind;
Substance to accident they turn with fire,
All to fulfill your gluttonous desire!
Out of the hard and riven bones knock they

80 The marrow, for they throw nothing away
That may go through the gullet soft and sweet;
With spicery, with leaf, bark, root, replete
Shall be the sauces made for your delight,
To furnish you a sharper appetite.

85 But truly, he that such delights entice
Is dead while yet he wallows in this vice.
A lecherous thing is wine, and drunkenness
Is full of striving and of wretchedness.
O drunken man, disfigured is your face,

90 Sour is your breath, foul are you to embrace,
And through your drunken nose there comes a sound
As if you snored out "Samson, Samson" round;
And yet God knows that Samson drank no wine.
You fall down just as if you were stuck swine;

95 Your tongue is loose, your honest care obscure;
For drunkenness is very sepulture[5]
Of any mind a man may chance to own.
In whom strong drink has domination shown
He can no counsel keep for any dread.

100 Now keep you from the white and from the red.
And specially from the white wine grown at Lepe[6]
That is for sale in Fish Street or in Cheap.[7]
This wine of Spain, it mixes craftily
With other wines that chance to be near by,

[5]*tomb*

[6]*a district in Spain where wine is grown*

[7]*two streets in*

London
[8]two wine-growing
districts in France

105 From which there rise such fumes, as well may be,
    That when a man has drunk two draughts, or three,
    And thinks himself to be at home in Cheap,
    He finds that he's in Spain, and right at Lepe,—
    Not at Rochelle nor yet at Bordeaux[8] town,
110 And then will he snore out "Samson, Samson."
    But hearken, masters, one word more I pray:
    The greatest deeds of all, I'm bold to say,
    Of victories in the old testament,
    Through the True God, Who is omnipotent,
115 Were gained by abstinence and after prayer:
    Look in the Bible, you may learn this there.
    Lo, Attila,[9] the mighty conqueror,
    Died in his sleep, in shame and dishonour,
    And bleeding at the nose for drunkenness;
120 A great captain should live in soberness.
    Above all this, advise yourself right well
    What was commanded unto Lemuel[10] —
    Not Samuel, but Lemuel, say I—
    The Bible's words you cannot well deny:
125 Drinking by magistrates is called a vice.
    No more of this, for it may well suffice.
        And now that I have told of gluttony,
    I'll take up gambling, showing you thereby
    The curse of chance, and all its evils treat;
130 From it proceeds false swearing and deceit,
    Blaspheming, murder, and—what's more—the waste
    Of time and money; add to which, debased
    And shamed and lost to honour quite is he,
    Who once a common gambler's known to be.
135 And ever the higher one is of estate,
    The more he's held disgraced and desolate.
    And if a prince plays similar hazardry
    In all his government and policy,
    He loses in the estimate of men
140 His good repute, and finds it not again.
    Chilon,[11] who was a wise ambassador,
    Was sent to Corinth,[12] all in great honour,
    From Lacedaemon,[13] to make alliance.
    And when he came, he noticed there, by chance,
145 All of the greatest people of the land

[9]the king of the
Huns who invaded
Europe in the 5th
century

[10]the biblical king
of Massa

[11]a Spartan politi-
cian and wise man

[12]a city in Greece

Playing at hazard there on every hand.
Wherefore, and all as soon as it might be,
He stole off home again to his country,
And said: "I will not thus debase my name;
150   Nor will I take upon me so great shame
You to ally with common hazarders.
Send, if you will, other ambassadors;
For, my truth, I say I'd rather die
Than you with gamblers like to them ally.
155   For you that are so glorious in honours
Shall never ally yourselves with hazarders
By my consent, or treaty I have made."
This wise philosopher, 'twas thus he said.
    Let us look, then, at King Demetrius.
160   The king of Parthia, as the book tells us,
Sent him a pair of golden dice, in scorn,
Because the name of gambler he had borne;
Wherefore he marked his reputation down
As valueless despite his wide renown.
165   Great lords may find sufficient other play
Seemly enough to while the time away.
Now will I speak of oaths both false and great
A word or two, whereof the old books treat.
Great swearing is a thing abominable,
170   And vain oaths yet more reprehensible. '
The High God did forbid swearing at all,
As witness Matthew;[14] but in especial
Of swearing says the holy Jeremiah,[15]
"Thou shalt not swear in vain, to be a liar,
175   But swear in judgment and in righteousness";
But idle swearing is a wickedness.
Behold, in the first table of the Law,
That should be honoured as High God's, sans flaw,
This second one of His commandments plain:
180   "Thou shalt not take the Lord God's name in vain."
Nay, sooner He forbids us such swearing
Than homicide or many a wicked thing;
I say that, as to order, thus it stands;
'tis known by him who His will understands
185   That the great second law of God is that.
Moreover, I will tell you full and flat,

[13]*Sparta*
[14]*the saint who wrote the first gospel*

That retribution will not quit his house
Who in his swearing is too outrageous.
"By God's own precious heart, and by His nails,
190 And by the blood of Christ that's now at Hales,[16]
Seven is my chance, and yours is five and trey!"
"By God's good arms, if you do falsely play,
This dagger through your heart I'll stick for you!"
Such is the whelping of the bitched bones two:
195 Perjury, anger, cheating, homicide.
Now for the love of Christ, Who for us died,
Forgo this swearing oaths, both great and small;
But, sirs, now will I tell to you my tale.
Now these three roisterers,[17] whereof I tell,
200 Long before prime[18] was rung by any bell,
Were sitting in a tavern for to drink;
And as they sat they heard a small bell clink
Before a corpse being carried to his grave;
Whereat one of them called unto his knave:
205 "Go run," said he, "and ask them civilly
What corpse it is that's just now passing by,
And see that you report the man's name well."
         "Sir," said the boy, "it needs not that they tell.
I learned it, ere you came here, full two hours;
210 He was, by gad, an old comrade of yours;
And he was slain, all suddenly, last night,
When drunk, as he sat on his bench upright;
An unseen thief, called Death, came stalking by,
Who hereabouts makes all the people die,
215 And with his spear he clove his heart in two
And went his way and made no more ado.
He's slain a thousand with this pestilence;
And, master, ere you come in his presence,
It seems to me to be right necessary
220 To be forewarned of such an adversary:
Be ready to meet him for evermore.
My mother taught me this, I say no more."
         "By holy Mary," said the innkeeper,
"The boy speaks truth, for Death has slain, this year,
225 A mile or more hence, in a large village,
Both man and woman, child and hind and page.
I think his habitation must be there;

[15] a biblical prophet
[16] an abbey in the southwest of England

[17] partyers

[18] nine a.m.

To be advised of him great wisdom 'twere,
Before he did a man some dishonour."
230   "Yea, by God's arms!" exclaimed this roisterer,
"Is it such peril, then, this Death to meet?
I'll seek him in the road and in the street,
As I now vow to God's own noble bones!
Hear, comrades, we're of one mind, as each owns;
235 Let each of us hold up his hand to other
And each of us become the other's brother,
And we three will go slay this traitor Death;
He shall be slain who's stopped so many a breath,
By God's great dignity, ere it be night."
240 Together did these three their pledges plight
To live and die, each of them for the other,
As if he were his very own blood brother.
And up they started, drunken, in this rage,
And forth they went, and towards that village
245 Whereof the innkeeper had told before.
And so, with many a grisly oath, they swore
And Jesus' blessed body once more rent—
"Death shall be dead if we find where he went."
When they had gone not fully half a mile,
250 Just as they would have trodden over a stile,
An old man, and a poor, with them did meet.
This ancient man full meekly them did greet,
And said thus: "Now, lords, God keep you and see!"
    The one that was most insolent of these three
255 Replied to him: "What? Churl of evil grace,
Why are you all wrapped up, except your face?
Why do you live so long in so great age?"
    This ancient man looked upon his visage
And thus replied: "Because I cannot find
260 A man, nay, though I walked from here to Ind,
Either in town or country who'll engage
To give his youth in barter for my age;
And therefore must I keep my old age still,
As long a time as it shall be God's will.
265 Not even Death, alas! my life will take;
Thus restless I my wretched way must make
And on the ground, which is my mother's gate,
I knock with my staff early, aye, and late,

And cry: 'O my dear mother, let me in!
270 Lo, how I'm wasted, flesh and blood and skin!
Alas! When shall my bones come to their rest?
Mother, with you fain would I change my chest,
That in my chamber so long time has been,
Aye! For a haircloth rag to wrap me in!'
275 But yet to me she will not show that grace,
And thus all pale and withered is my face.
    "But, sirs, in you it is no courtesy
To speak to an old man despitefully,
Unless in word he trespass or in deed.
280 In holy writ you may, yourselves, well read
'Before an old man, hoar[19] upon the head,
You should arise.' Which I advise you read,
Nor to an old man any injury do
More than you would that men should do to you
285 In age, if you so long time shall abide;
And God be with you, whether you walk or ride.
I must pass on now where I have to go."
    "Nay, ancient churl, by God it sha'n't be so,"
Cried out this other hazarder, anon;
290 "You sha'n't depart so easily, by Saint John!
You spoke just now of that same traitor Death,
Who in this country stops our good friends' breath
Hear my true word, since you are his own spy,
Tell where he is or you shall rue it, aye
295 By God and by the holy Sacrament!
Indeed you must be, with this Death, intent
To slay all us young people, you false thief."
    "Now, sirs," said he, "if you're so keen, in brief,
to find out Death, turn up this crooked way,
300 For in that grove I left him, by my fay,
Under a tree, and there he will abide;
Nor for your boasts will he a moment hide.
See you that oak? Right there you shall him find.
God save you, Who redeemed all humankind,
305 And mend your ways!"—thus said this ancient man.
And every one of these three roisterers ran
Till he came to that tree; and there they found,
Of florins[20] of fine gold, new-minted, round,
Well-nigh eight bushels full, or so they thought.

[19]*white*

[20]*coins*

310 No longer, then, after this Death they sought,
    But each of them so glad was of that sight,
    Because the florins were so fair and bright,
    That down they all sat by this precious hoard.
    The worst of them was first to speak a word.
315 "Brothers," said he, "take heed to what I say;
    My wits are keen, although I mock and play.
    This treasure here Fortune to us has given
    That mirth and jollity our lives may liven,
    And easily as it's come, so will we spend.
320 Eh! By God's precious dignity! Who'd pretend,
    Today, that we should have so fair a grace
    But might this gold be carried from this place
    Home to my house, or if you will, to yours—
    For well we know that all this gold is ours—
325 Then were we all in high felicity.
    But certainly by day this may not be;
    For men would say that we were robbers strong,
    And we'd, for our own treasure, hang ere long.
    This treasure must be carried home by night
330 All prudently and slyly, out of sight.
    So I propose that cuts among us all
    Be drawn, and let's see where the cut will fall;
    And he that gets the short cut, blithe of heart
    Shall run to town at once, and to the mart,
335 And fetch us bread and wine here, privately.
    And two of us shall guard, right cunningly,
    This treasure well; and if he does not tarry,
    When it is night we'll all the treasure carry
    Where, by agreement, we may think it best."
340 That one of them the cuts brought in his fist
    And bade them draw to see where it might fall;
    And it fell on the youngest of them all;
    And so, forth toward the town he went anon.
    And just as soon as he had turned and gone,
345 That one of them spoke thus unto the other:
    "You know well that you are my own sworn brother,
    So to your profit I will speak anon.
    You know well how our comrade is just gone;
    And here is gold, and that in great plenty,
350 That's to be parted here among us three.

Nevertheless, if I can shape it so
That it be parted only by us two,
Shall I not do a turn that is friendly?"
    The other said: "Well, now, how can that be?
355 He knows well that the gold is with us two.
What shall we say to him? What shall we do?"
    "Shall it be secret?" asked the first rogue, then,
"And I will tell you in eight words, or ten,
What we must do, and how bring it about."
360   "Agreed," replied the other, "Never doubt,
That, on my word, I nothing will betray."
    "Now," said the first, "we're two, and I dare say
The two of us are stronger than is one.
Watch when he sits, and soon as that is done
365 Arise and make as if with him to play;
And I will thrust him through the two sides, yea,
The while you romp with him as in a game,
And with your dagger see you do the same;
And then shall all this gold divided be,
370 My right dear friend, just between you and me;
Then may we both our every wish fulfill
And play at dice all at our own sweet will."
And thus agreed were these two rogues, that day,
To slay the third, as you have heard me say.
375   This youngest rogue who'd gone into the town,
Often in fancy rolled he up and down
The beauty of those florins new and bright.
"O Lord," thought he, "if so be that I might
Have all this treasure to myself alone,
380 There is no man who lives beneath the throne
Of God that should be then so merry as I."
    And at the last the Fiend, our enemy,
Put in his thought that he should poison buy
With which he might kill both his fellows; aye,
385 The Devil found him in such wicked state,
He had full leave his grief to consummate;
For it was utterly the man's intent
To kill them both and never to repent.
And on he strode, no longer would he tarry,
390 Into the town, to an apothecary,[21]
And prayed of him that he'd prepare and sell

Some poison for his rats, and some as well
For a polecat[22] that in his yard had lain,
The which, he said, his capons[23] there had slain,
395 And fain[24] he was to rid him, if he might,
Of vermin that thus damaged him by night.
The apothecary said: "And you shall have
A thing of which, so God my spirit save,
In all this world there is not live creature
400 That's eaten or has drunk of this mixture
As much as equals but a grain of wheat,
That shall not sudden death thereafter meet;
Yea, die he shall, and in a shorter while
Than you require to walk but one short mile;
405 This poison is so violent and strong."
This wicked man the poison took along
With him boxed up, and then he straightway ran
Into the street adjoining, to a man,
And of him borrowed generous bottles three;
410 And into two his poison then poured he;
The third one he kept clean for his own drink.
For all that night he was resolved to swink[25]
In carrying the florins from that place.
And when this roisterer, with evil grace,
415 Had filled with wine his mighty bottles three,
Then to his comrades forth again went he.
What is the need to tell about it more?
For just as they had planned his death before,
Just so they murdered him, and that anon.
420 And when the thing was done, then spoke the one:
"Now let us sit and drink and so be merry,
And afterward we will his body bury."
And as he spoke, one bottle of the three
He took wherein the poison chanced to be
425 And drank and gave his comrade drink also,
For which, and that anon, lay dead these two.
I feel quite sure that Doctor Avicena[26]
Within the sections of his Canon never
Set down more certain signs of poisoning
430 Than showed these wretches two at their ending.
Thus ended these two homicides in woe;
Died thus the treacherous poisoner also.

[21]*pharmacist*
[22]*skunk*

[23]*young chickens*

[24]*eager*

[25]*work*

[26]*Avicenna, an author of a medical treatise*

O cursed sin, full of abominableness!

O treacherous homicide! O wickedness!

435 O gluttony, lechery, and hazardry!

O blasphemer of Christ with villainy,

And with great oaths, habitual for pride!

Alas! Mankind, how may this thing betide[27]

That to thy dear Creator, Who thee wrought,

440 And with His precious blood salvation bought,

Thou art so false and so unkind, alas!

Now, good men, God forgive you each trespass,

And keep you from the sin of avarice.[28]

My holy pardon cures and will suffice,

445 So that it brings me gold, or silver brings,

Or else, I care not—brooches, spoons or rings.

Bow down your heads before this holy bull!

Come up, you wives, and offer of your wool!

Your names I'll enter on my roll, anon,

450 And into Heaven's bliss you'll go, each one.

For I'll absolve you, by my special power,

You that make offering, as clean this hour

As you were born.

              And lo, sirs, thus I preach.

455 And Jesus Christ, who is our souls' great leech,[29]

So grant you each his pardon to receive;

For that is best; I will not you deceive.

But, sirs, one word forgot I in my tale;

I've relics in my pouch that cannot fail,

460 As good as England ever saw, I hope,

The which I got by kindness of the pope.

If gifts your change of heart and mind reveal.

You'll get my absolution while you kneel.

Come forth, and kneel down here before, anon.

465 And humbly you'll receive my full pardon;

Or else receive a pardon as you wend,

All new and fresh as every mile shall end,

So that you offer me each time, anew,

More gold and silver, all good coins and true.

470 It is an honour to each one that's here

That you may have a competent pardoner

To give you absolution as you ride,

For all adventures that may still betide.

[27]*happen*

[28]*eagerness for money; greed*

[29]*healer*

Perchance from horse may fall down one or two,
475 Breaking his neck, and it might well be you.
See what insurance, then, it is for all
That I within your fellowship did fall,
Who may absolve you, both the great and less,
When soul from body passes, as I guess.
480 I think our host might just as well begin,
For he is most enveloped in all sin.
Come forth, sir host, and offer first anon,
And you shall kiss the relics, every one,
Aye, for a groat![30] Unbuckle now your purse."

[30]*coin*

485 "Nay, nay," said he, "then may I have Christ's curse!
It sha'n't be," said he, "as I've hope for riches,
Why, you would have me kissing your old breeches,
And swear they were the relics of a saint,
Though with your excrement 'twere dabbed like paint.
490 By cross Saint Helen found in Holy Land,
I would I had your ballocks in my hand
Instead of relics in a reliquary;
Let's cut them off, and them I'll help you carry;
They shall be shrined within a hog's fat turd."
495 This pardoner, he answered not a word;
So wrathy[31] was he no word would he say.
    "Now," said our host, "I will no longer play
With you, nor any other angry man."
But at this point the worthy knight began,

[31]*angry*

500 When that he saw how all the folk did laugh:
"No more of this, for it's gone far enough;
Sir pardoner, be glad and merry here;
And you, sir host, who are to me so dear,
I pray you that you kiss the pardoner.
505 And, pardoner, I pray you to draw near,
And as we did before, let's laugh and play."
And then they kissed and rode forth on their way.

The *Nun's Priest's*

P R O L O G U E

"HOLD!" cried the knight. "Good sir, no more of this,[1]
What you have said is right enough, and is
Very much more; a little heaviness
Is plenty for the most of us, I guess.
5 For me, I say it's saddening, if you please,
As to men who've enjoyed great wealth and ease,
To hear about their sudden fall, alas,
But the contrary's joy and great solace,
As when a man has been in poor estate
10 And he climbs up and waxes fortunate,
And there abides in all prosperity.
Such things are gladsome, as it seems to me,
And of such things it would be good to tell."
    "Yea, quoth our host, "and by Saint Paul's[2] great bell,
15 You say the truth; this monk, his clapper's loud.
He spoke how 'Fortune covered with a cloud'
I know not what, and of a 'tragedy,'
As now you heard, and gad! no remedy
It is to wail and wonder and complain
20 That certain things have happened, and it's pain.
As you have said, to hear of wretchedness.
Sir monk, no more of this, so God you bless!

[1] *The monk has just finished giving different examples of the fall of great men.*

[2] *a major cathedral in London*

167

Your tale annoys the entire company;
Such talking is not worth a butterfly;
25 For in it is no sport nor any game.
Wherefore, sir monk, Sir Peter by your name,
I pray you heartily tell us something else,
For truly, but for clinking of the bells
That from your bridle hang on either side,
30 By Heaven's king, Who for us all has died,
I should, ere this, have fallen down for sleep,
Although the mud had never been so deep;
Then had your story all been told in vain.
For certainly, as all these clerks complain,
35 'Whenas a man has none for audience,
It's little help to speak his evidence.'
And well I know the substance is in me
To judge of things that well reported be.
Sir, tell a tale of hunting now, I pray."
40   "Nay," said this monk, "I have no wish to play;
Now let another tell, as I have told."
       Then spoke our host out, in rude speech and bold,
And said he unto the nun's priest anon:
"Come near, you priest, come hither, you Sir John,
45 Tell us a thing to make our hearts all glad;
Be blithe, although you ride upon a jade.
What though your horse may be both foul and lean?
If he but serves you, why, don't care a bean;
Just see your heart is always merry. So."
50   "Yes, sir," said he, "yes, host, so may I go,
For, save I'm merry, I know I'll be blamed."
And right away his story has he framed,
And thus he said unto us, every one,
This dainty priest, this goodly man, Sir John.

The
Nun's Priest's
TALE

OF THE COCK AND HEN:
CHANTICLEER AND PERTELOTE

A WIDOW poor, somewhat advanced in age,
Lived, on a time, within a small cottage
Beside a grove and standing down a dale.
This widow, now, of whom I tell my tale,
5 Since that same day when she'd been last a wife,
Had led, with patience, her straight simple life,
For she'd small goods and little income-rent;
By husbanding[1] of such as God had sent
She kept herself and her young daughters twain.
10 Three large sows had she, and no more, 'tis plain,
Three cows and a lone sheep that she called Moll.
Right sooty was her bedroom and her hall,
Wherein she'd eaten many a slender meal.
Of sharp sauce, why she needed no great deal,
15 For dainty morsel never passed her throat;
Her diet well accorded with her cote.[2]
Repletion never made this woman sick;
A temperate diet was her whole physic,[3]
And exercise, and her heart's sustenance.
20 The gout, it hindered her nothing to dance,
Nor apoplexy spun within her head;
And no wine drank she,—either white or red;

[1] managing

[2] small shed (i.e.,
Her eating habits
matched her
modest home.)

[3] medicine

169

Her board was mostly garnished, white and black,
With milk and brown bread, whereof she'd no lack,
25 Broiled bacon and sometimes an egg or two,
For a small dairy business did she do.
    A yard she had, enclosed all roundabout
With pales,[4] and there was a dry ditch without,
And in the yard a cock called Chanticleer.
30 In all the land, for crowing, he'd no peer.
His voice was merrier than the organ gay
On Mass days, which in church begins to play;
More regular was his crowing in his lodge
Than is a clock or abbey horologe.[5]
35 By instinct he'd marked each ascension down
Of equinoctial value in that town;[6]
And when fifteen degrees[7] had been ascended,
Then crew he so it might not be amended.
His comb was redder than a fine coral,
40 And battlemented like a castle wall.
His bill was black and just like jet it shone;
Like azure were his legs and toes, each one;
His spurs were whiter than the lily flower;
And like burnished gold was his color.
45 This noble cock had in his governance
Seven hens to give him pride and all pleasance,
Which were his sisters and his paramours[8]
And wondrously like him as to colours,
Whereof the fairest hued upon her throat
50 Was called the winsome Mistress Pertelote.
Courteous she was, discreet and debonnaire,
Companionable, and she had been so fair
Since that same day when she was seven nights old,
That truly she had taken the heart to hold
55 Of Chanticleer, locked in every limb;
He loved her so that all was well with him.
But such a joy it was to hear them sing,
Whenever the bright sun began to spring,
In sweet accord, "My love walks through the land."
60 For at that time, and as I understand,
The beasts and all the birds could speak and sing
    So it befell that, in a bright dawning,

[4]fence posts

[5]clock

[6]By instinct, he
knew the time.

[7]measurements of
Earth's movement
by which time
was calculated

[8]mistresses

As Chanticleer 'midst wives and sisters all
Sat on his perch, the which was in the hall,
65 And next him sat the winsome Pertelote,
This Chanticleer he groaned within his throat
Like man that in his dreams is troubled sore.
And when fair Pertelote thus heard him roar,
She was aghast and said: "O sweetheart dear,
70 What ails you that you groan so? Do you hear?
You are a sleepy herald. Fie, for shame!"
    And he replied to her thus: "Ah, madame,
I pray you that you take it not in grief,
By God. I dreamed I'd come to such mischief,
75 Just now, my heart yet jumps with sore affright.
Now God," cried he, "my vision read aright
And keep my body out of foul prison!
I dreamed, that while I wandered up and down
Within our yard, I saw there a strange beast
80 Was like a dog, and he'd have made a feast
Upon my body, and have had me dead.
His colour yellow was and somewhat red;
And tipped his tail was, as were both his ears,
With black, unlike the rest, as it appears;
85 His snout was small and gleaming was each eye.
Remembering how he looked, almost I die;
And all this caused my groaning, I confess."
    "Aha," said she, "fie on you, spiritless!
Alas!" cried she, "for by that God above,
90 Now have you lost my heart and all my love;
I cannot love a coward, by my faith.
For truly, whatsoever woman saith,
We all desire, if only it may be,
To have a husband hardy, wise, and free.
95 And trustworthy, no niggard, and no fool,
Nor one that is afraid of every tool,
Nor yet a braggart, by that God above!
How dare you say, for shame, unto your love
That there is anything that you have feared?
100 Have you not man's heart, and yet have a beard?
Alas! And are you frightened by a vision?
Dreams are, God knows, a matter for derision.

Visions are generated by repletions
And vapours and the body's bad secretions."9
105 Of humours overabundant in a wight.
Surely this dream, which you have had tonight,
Comes only of the superfluity10
Of your bilious11 irascibility,12
Which causes folk to shiver in their dreams
110 For arrows and for flames with long red gleams,
For great beasts in the fear that they will bite,
For quarrels and for wolf whelps great and slight;
Just as the humour of melancholy
Causes full many a man, in sleep, to cry,
115 For fear of black bears or of bulls all black,
Or lest black devils put them in a sack.
Of other humours could I tell also,
That bring, to many a sleeping man, great woe;
But I'll pass on as lightly as I can.
120   "Lo, Cato,13 and he was a full wise man,
Said he not, we should trouble not for dreams?
Now, sir," said she, "when we fly from the beams,
For God's love go and take some laxative;
On peril of my soul, and as I live,
125 I counsel you the best, I will not lie.
That both for choler14 and for melancholy15
You purge16 yourself; and since you shouldn't tarry,
And on this farm there's no apothecary,
I will myself go find some herbs for you
130 That will be good for health and pecker too;
And in our own yard all these herbs I'll find,
The which have properties of proper kind
To purge you underneath and up above.
Forget this not, now, for God's very love!
135 You are so very choleric of complexion.
Beware the mounting sun and all dejection,
Nor get yourself with sudden humours hot;
For if you do, I dare well lay a groat
That you shall have the tertian fever's17 pain,
140 Or some ague that may well be your bane.18
A day or two you shall have digestives
Of worms before you take your laxatives

9An imbalance of certain bodily fluids was supposed to cause mood disorders and bad dreams.

10overabundance

11having excess bile

12irritability

13a Roman author whose works were often cited in the medieval period

14irritability

15depression

16purify, usually through the expulsion of harmful elements

17a fever that happens every other day

18curse; destruction

Of laurel, centuary, and fumitory,
Or else of hellebore purificatory,
145 Or caper spurge,[19] or else of dogwood berry,
Or herb ivy, all in our yard so merry;
Peck them just as they grow and gulp them in.
Be merry, husband, for your father's kin!
Dread no more dreams. And I can say no more."
150 "Madam," said he, "gramercy[20] for your lore.
Nevertheless, not running Cato down,
Who had for wisdom such a high renown,
And though he says to hold no dreams in dread,
By God, men have, in many old books, read
155 Of many a man more an authority
That ever Cato was, pray pardon me,
Who say just the reverse of his sentence,
And have found out by long experience
That dreams, indeed, are good significations,
160 As much of joys as of all tribulations
That folk endure here in this life present.
There is no need to make an argument;
The very proof of this is shown indeed."
    "One of the greatest authors that men read
165 Says thus: That on a time two comrades went
On pilgrimage, and all in good intent;
And it so chanced they came into a town
Where there was such a crowding, up and down
Of people, and so little harbourage,
170 That they found not so much as one cottage
Wherein the two of them might sheltered be.
Wherefore they must, as of necessity,
For that one night at least, part company;
And each went to a different hostelry
175 And took such lodgment as to him did fall.
Now one of them was lodged within a stall,
Far in a yard, with oxen of the plow;
That other man found shelter fair enow,[21]
As was his luck, or was his good fortune,
180 Whatever 'tis that governs us, each one."
    "So it befell that, long ere it was day,
This last man dreamed in bed, as there he lay,

That his poor fellow did unto him call,
Saying: 'Alas! For in an ox's stall
185 This night shall I be murdered where I lie.
Now help me, brother dear, before I die.
Come in all haste to me. 'Twas that he said.
This man woke out of sleep, then, all afraid;
But when he'd wakened fully from his sleep,
190 He turned upon his pillow, yawning deep,
Thinking his dream was but a fantasy.
And then again, while sleeping, thus dreamed he.
And then a third time came a voice that said
(Or so he thought): 'Now, comrade, I am dead;
195 Behold my bloody wounds, so wide and deep!
Early arise tomorrow from your sleep,
And at the west gate of the town,' said he,
'A wagon full of dung there shall you see,
Wherein is hid my body craftily;
200 Do you arrest this wagon right boldly.
They killed me for what money they could gain.'
And told in every point how he'd been slain,
With a most pitiful face and pale of hue.
And trust me well, this dream did all come true; .
205 For on the morrow, soon as it was day,
Unto his comrade's inn he took the way;
And when he'd come into that ox's stall
Upon his fellow he began to call."

        "The keeper of the place replied anon,
210 And said he: 'Sir, your friend is up and gone;
As soon as day broke he went out of town.'
This man, then, felt suspicion in him grown,
Remembering the dream that he had had,
And forth he went, no longer tarrying, sad,
215 Unto the west gate-of the town, and found
A dung-cart on its way to dumping-ground,
And it was just the same in every wise
As you have heard the dead man advertise;
And with a hardy heart he then did cry
220 Vengeance and justice on this felony:
'My comrade has been murdered in the night,
And in this very cart lies, face upright.

I cry to all the officers,' said he
'That ought to keep the peace in this city.
225 Alas, alas, here lies my comrade slain!'"
        "Why should I longer with this tale detain?
The people rose and turned the cart to ground,
And in the center of the dung they found
The dead man, lately murdered in his sleep."
230   "O Blessed God, Who art so true and deep!
Lo, how Thou dost turn murder out alway!
Murder will out, we see it every day.
Murder's so hateful and abominable
To God, Who is so just and reasonable,
235 That He'll not suffer that it hidden be;
Though it may skulk a year, or two, or three,
Murder will out, and I conclude thereon.
Immediately the rulers of that town,
They took the carter and so sore they racked
240 Him and the host, until their bones were cracked,
That they confessed their wickedness anon,
And hanged they both were by the neck, and soon.
"Here may men see that dreams are things to dread.
And certainly, in that same book I read,
245 Right in the very chapter after this
(I spoof not, as I may have joy and bliss),
Of two men who would voyage oversea,
For some cause, and unto a far country,
If but the winds had not been all contrary,
250 Causing them both within a town to tarry,
Which town was builded near the haven-side.
But then, one day, along toward eventide,
The wind did change and blow as suited best.
Jolly and glad they went unto their rest.
255 And were prepared right early for to sail;
But unto one was told a marvelous tale.
For one of them, a-sleeping as he lay,
Did dream a wondrous dream ere it was day.
He thought a strange man stood by his bedside
260 And did command him, he should there abide,
And said to him: 'If you tomorrow wend,
You shall be drowned; my tale is at an end.'

He woke and told his fellow what he'd met
And prayed him quit the voyage and forget;
265 For just one day he prayed him there to bide.
His comrade, who was lying there beside,
Began to laugh and scorned him long and fast.
"'No dream,' said he, 'may make my heart aghast,
So that I'll quit my business for such things.
270 I do not care a straw for your dreamings,
For visions are but fantasies and japes.
Men dream, why, every day, of owls and apes,
And many a wild phantasm therewithal;
Men dream of what has never been, nor shall.
275 But since I see that you will here abide,
And thus forgo this fair wind and this tide,
God knows I'm sorry; nevertheless, good day!'
    "And thus he took his leave and went his way.
But long before the half his course he'd sailed,
280 I know not why, nor what it was that failed,
But casually the vessel's bottom rent,
And ship and men under the water went,
In sight of other ships were there beside,
The which had sailed with that same wind and tide.
285 And therefore, pretty Pertelote, my dear,
By such an old example may you hear
And learn that no man should be too reckless
Of dreams, for I can tell you, fair mistress,
That many a dream is something well to dread.
290   "Why in the 'Life' of Saint Kenelm[22] I read
(Who was Kenelphus' son, the noble king
Of Mercia), how Kenelm dreamed a thing;
A while ere he was murdered, so they say,
His own death in a vision saw, one day.
295 His nurse interpreted, as records tell,
That vision, bidding him to guard him well
From treason; but he was but seven years old,
And therefore 'twas but little he'd been told
Of any dream, so holy was his heart.
300 By God! I'd rather than retain my shirt
That you had read this legend, as have I.
Dame Pertelote, I tell you verily,

[22]*the young king of Mercia who dreamed about his murder before it was committed*

Macrobius,[23] who wrote of Scipio[24]
The African a vision long ago,

305　He holds by dreams, saying that they have been
Warnings of things that men have later seen.
　　　"And furthermore, I pray you to look well
In the Old Testament at Daniel,[25]
Whether he held dreams for mere vanity.

310　Read, too, of Joseph,[26] and you there shall see
Where dreams have sometimes been (I say not all)
Warnings of things that, after did befall.
Consider Egypt's king, Sir Pharaoh,
His baker and his butler, these also,

315　Whether they knew of no effect from dreams.
Whoso will read of sundry realms the themes
May learn of dreams full many a wondrous thing.
Lo, Croesus, who was once of Lydia king,
Dreamed he not that he sat upon a tree,

320　Which signified that hanged high he should be?
Lo, how Andromache, great Hector's wife,
On that same day when Hector lost his life,
She dreamed upon the very night before
That Hector's life should be lost evermore,

325　If on that day he battled, without fail.
She warned him, but no warning could avail;
He went to fight, despite all auspices,[27]
And so was shortly slain by Achilles.
But that same tale is all too long to tell,

330　And, too, it's nearly day, I must not dwell
Upon this point I say; concluding here,
That from this vision I have cause to fear
Adversity; and I say, furthermore,
That I do set by laxatives no store,

335　For they are poisonous, I know it well.
Them I defy and love not, truth to tell."
　　　"But let us speak of mirth and stop all this;
My lady Pertelote, on hope of bliss,
In one respect God's given me much grace;

340　For when I see the beauty of your face,
You are so rosy-red beneath each eye,
It makes my dreadful terror wholly die.

[23]*the Roman author who wrote a commentary on Cicero's Dream of Scipio*

[24]*Scipio Africanus, who dreamed he was shown the earth, the heavens, and the universe*

[25]*the biblical figure who prophesized the future of the Jews*

[26]*the biblical figure who interpreted the Pharaoh's dreams*

[27]*predictions of future events*

For there is truth in In principio
Mulier est hominis confusio
345 (Madam, the meaning of this latin is,
Woman is man's delight and all his bliss).
For when I feel at night your tender side,
Although I cannot then upon you ride,
Because our perch so narrow is, alas!
350 I am so full of joy and all solace
That I defy, then, vision, aye and dream."
And with that word he flew down from the beam,
For it was day, and down went his hens all;
And with a cluck he them began to call,
355 For he had found some corn within the yard.
Regal he was, and fears he did discard.
He feathered Pertelote full many a time
And twenty times he trod her ere 'twas prime
He looked as if he were a grim lion
360 As on his toes he strutted up and-down;
He deigned not set his foot upon the ground.
He clucked when any grain of corn he found,
And all his wives came running at his call.
Thus regal, as prince is in his hall,
365 I'll now leave busy Chanticleer to feed,
And with events that followed I'll proceed.

When that same month wherein the world began,
Which is called March, wherein God first made man,
Was ended, and were passed of days also
370 Since March began, full thirty days and two,
It fell that Chanticleer, in all his pride,
His seven wives a-walking by his side,
Cast up his two eyes toward the great bright sun.
(Which through the sign of Taurus now had run
375 Twenty degrees and one, and somewhat more),
And knew by instinct and no other lore

That it was prime, and joyfully he crew,[28]
"The sun, my love," he said, "has climbed anew.
Forty degrees and one, and somewhat more.
380 My lady Pertelote, whom I adore,
Mark now these happy birds, hear how they sing.
And see all these fresh flowers, how they spring;
Full is my heart of revelry and grace."

But suddenly he fell in grievous case;
385   For ever the latter end of joy is woe.
God knows that wordly joys do swiftly go.
And if a rhetorician could but write,
He in some chronicle might well indite[29]
And mark it down as sovereign[30] in degree.
390   Now every wise man, let him hark to me:
This tale is just as true, I undertake,
As is the book of Launcelot of the Lake,[31]
Which women always hold in such esteem.
But now I must take up my proper theme.
395   A brant[32]-fox, full of sly iniquity,
That in the grove had lived two years, or three,
Now by a fine premeditated plot
That same night, breaking through the hedge, had got
Into the yard where Chanticleer the fair
400   Was wont, and all his wives too, to repair;
And in a bed of greenery still he lay
Till it was past the quarter[33] of the day,
Waiting his chance on Chanticleer to fall.
As gladly do these killers one and all
405   Who lie in ambush for to murder men.
O murderer false, there lurking in your den!
O new Iscariot,[34] O new Ganelon![35]
O false dissimulator,[36] Greek Sinon[37]
That brought down Troy all utterly to sorrow!
410   O Chanticleer, accursed be that morrow
When you into that yard flew from the beams!
You were well warned, and fully, by your dreams
That this day should hold peril damnably.
But that which God foreknows, it needs must be.
415   So says the best opinion of the clerks.
Witness some cleric perfect for his works,
That in the schools there's a great altercation[38]
In this regard, and much high disputation[39]
That has involved a hundred thousand men.
420   But I can't sift it to the bran with pen,[40]
As can the holy Doctor Augustine,[41]
Or Boethius, or Bishop Bradwardine,[42]
Whether the fact of God's great foreknowing[43]
Makes it right needful that I do a thing

[29]compose

[30]noteworthy

[31]the story of Lancelot and Guinevere

[32]brown

[33]i.e., it was about nine a.m.

[34]Judas Iscariot, the man who betrayed Christ

[35]the man who betrayed the nephew of Charlemagne, Roland

[36]deceiver

[37]the man who had the Trojan Horse brought to Troy

[38]argument

[39]debate

[40]separate truth from incorrect information

[41]St. Augustine, who said that God granted man freewill

[42]Thomas Bradwardyn, who argued that every occurrence in life is predestined by God

[43]Chanticleer refers to a common religious debate over whether humans (or roosters) are given free will.

425 (By needful, I mean, of necessity);
    Or else, if a free choice he granted me,
    To do that same thing, or to do it not,
    Though God foreknew before the thing was wrought;
    Or if His knowing constrains never at all,
430 Save by necessity conditional.
    I have no part in matters so austere;
    My tale is of a cock, as you shall hear,
    That took the counsel of his wife, with sorrow,
    To walk within the yard upon that morrow
435 After he'd had the dream whereof I told.
    Now women's counsels oft are ill to hold;
    A woman's counsel brought us first to woe,
    And Adam caused from Paradise to go,
    Wherein he was right merry and at ease.
440 But since I know not whom it may displease
    If woman's counsel I hold up to blame,
    Pass over, I but said it in my game.
    Read authors where such matters do appear,
    And what they say of women, you may hear.
445 These are the cock's words, they are none of mine;[44]
    No harm in women can I e'er divine.
      All in the sand, a-bathing merrily,
    Lay Pertelote, with all her sisters by,
    There in the sun; and Chanticleer so free
450 Sang merrier than mermaid in the sea
    (For Physiologus[45] says certainly
    That they do sing, both well and merrily).
    And so befell that, as he cast his eye
    Among the herbs and on a butterfly,
455 He saw this fox that lay there, crouching low.
    Nothing of urge was in him, then, to crow;
    But he cried "Cock-cock-cock" and did so start
    As man who has a sudden fear at heart.
    For naturally a beast desires to flee
460 From any enemy that he may see.
    Though never yet he's clapped on such his eye.
    When Chanticleer the fox did then espy,
    He would have fled but that the fox anon
    Said: "Gentle sir, alas! Why be thus gone?
465 Are you afraid of me, who am your friend?

[44] an ironic statement on Chaucer's part

[45] an invented medical authority

Now surely, I were worse than any fiend
If I should do you harm or villainy.
I came not here upon your deeds to spy;
But, certainly, the cause of my coming
470 Was only just to listen to you sing.
For truly, you have quite as fine a voice
As angels have that Heaven's choirs rejoice.
Boethius to music could not bring
Such feeling, nor do others who can sing.
475 My lord your father (God his soul pray bless!)
And too your mother, of her gentleness,
Have been in my abode, to my great ease;
And truly, sir, right fain am I to please.
But since men speak of singing, I will say
480 (As I still have my eyesight day by day),
Save you, I never heard a man so sing
As did your father in the grey dawning;
Truly 'twas from the heart, his every song.
And that his voice might ever be more strong,
485 He took such pains that, with his either eye
He had to blink, so loudly would he cry,
A-standing on his tiptoes therewithal,
Stretching his neck till it grew long and small.
And such discretion, too, by him was shown,
490 There was no man in any region known
That him in song or wisdom could surpass.
I have well read, in Sir Burnell the Ass,[46]
Among his verses, how there was a cock,
Because a priest's son gave to him a knock
495 Upon the leg, while young and not yet wise,
He caused the boy to lose his benefice.
But, truly, there is no comparison
With the great wisdom and the discretion
Your father had, or with his subtlety.
500 Now sing, dear sir, for holy charity,
See if you can your father counterfeit."
    This Chanticleer his wings began to beat,
As one that could no treason there espy,
So was he ravished by this flattery.
505 Alas, you lords! Full many a flatterer
Is in your courts, and many a cozener,[47]

[46] *a popular satire*

[47] *cheater*

That please your honours much more, by my fay,
Than he that truth and justice dares to say.

48the author
of the book of
Ecclesiastes, in the
Bible

Go read the Ecclesiast[48] on flattery;
510 Beware, my lords, of all their treachery!
    This Chanticleer stood high upon his toes,
Stretching his neck, and both his eyes did close,
And so did crow right loudly, for the nonce;

49a typical name
for a fox in fables
and parables

50throat

And Russel[49] Fox, he started up at once,
515 And by the gorget[50] grabbed our Chanticleer,
Flung him on back, and toward the wood did steer,
For there was no man who as yet pursued.
O destiny, you cannot be eschewed!
Alas, that Chanticleer flew from the beams!
520 Alas, his wife recked nothing of his dreams!
And on a Friday fell all this mischance.
O Venus, who art goddess of pleasance,
Since he did serve thee well, this Chanticleer,
And to the utmost of his power here,

51Geoffrey of
Vinsauf, who
wrote a lament
on the death
of Richard the
Lionheart

52Richard I,
leader of the
Third Crusade
and who was king
of England from
1189 to 1199

53desolation

54the son of
Achilles, who
killed Priam at the
siege of Troy

55father of Hector
and king of Troy

56a work written
by Virgil about the
hero Aeneus, the
fall of Troy, and
the founding of
Rome

57a Carthaginian
general who
fought in the
Second Punic War

525 More for delight than cocks to multiply,
Why would'st thou suffer him that day to die?
O Gaufred,[51] my dear master sovereign,
Who, when King Richard Lionheart[52] was slain
By arrow, sang his death with sorrow sore,
530 Why have I not your faculty and lore
To chide Friday, as you did worthily?
(For truly, on a Friday slain was he).
Then would I prove how well I could complain
For Chanticleer's great fear and all his pain.
535 Certainly no such cry and lamentation
Were made by ladies at Troy's debolation,[53]
When Pyrrhus[54] with his terrible bared sword
Had taken old King Priam[55] by the beard
And slain him (as the Aeneid[56] tells to us),
540 As made then all those hens in one chorus
When they had caught a sight of Chanticleer.
But fair Dame Pertelote assailed the ear
Far louder than did Hasdrubal's[57] good wife
When that her husband bold had lost his life,
545 And Roman legionaries burned Carthage;
For she so full of torment was, and rage,
She voluntarily to the fire did start

And burned herself there with a steadfast heart.
And you, O woeful hens, just so you cried
550 As when base Nero burned the city wide
Of Rome, and wept the senators' stern wives
Because their husbands all had lost their lives,
For though not guilty, Nero had them slain.
Now will I turn back to my tale again.

555 This simple widow and her daughters two
Heard these hens cry and make so great ado,
And out of doors they started on the run
And saw the fox into the grove just gone,
Bearing in his mouth the cock away.
560 And then they cried, "Alas, and weladay!
Oh, the fox!" and after him they ran,
And after them, with staves, went many a man;
Ran Coll, our dog, and Talbot and Garland,
Ran cow and calf and even the very hogs,
565 So were they scared by barking of the dogs
And shouting men and women all did make,
They all ran so they thought their hearts would break.
And now, good men, I pray you hearken all.
They yelled as very fiends do down in Hell;
570 The ducks they cried as at the butcher fell;
The frightened geese flew up above the trees;
Out of the hive there came the swarm of bees;
So terrible was the noise, ah ben'cite!
Certainly old Jack Straw[58] and his army
575 Never raised shouting half so loud and shrill
When they were chasing Flemings for to kill,
As on that day was raised upon the fox.
They brought forth trumpets made of brass, of box,
Of horn, of bone, wherein they blew and pooped,
580 And therewithal they screamed and shrieked and whooped;
It seemed as if the heaven itself should fall!
Behold how Fortune turns all suddenly
The hope and pride of even her enemy!
This cock, which now lay in the fox's mouth,
585 In all his fear unto the fox did clack
And say: "Sir, were I you, as I should be,
Then would I say (as God may now help me!),
'Turn back again, presumptuous peasants all!

[58]*the leader of the 1381 Peasants' Revolt*

A very pestilence upon you fall!
590 Now that I've gained here to this dark wood's side,
In spite of you this cock shall here abide.
I'll eat him, by my faith, and that anon!'"
The fox replied: "In faith, it shall be done!"
And as he spoke that word, all suddenly
595 This cock broke from his mouth, full cleverly,
And high upon a tree he flew anon.
And when the fox saw well that he was gone,
"Alas," quoth he, "O Chanticleer, alas!
I have against you done a base trespass
600 Inasmuch as I made you afeared
When I seized you and brought you from the yard;
But, sir, I did it with no foul intent;
Come down, and I will tell you what I meant.
I'll tell the truth to you, God help me so!
605   "Nay then," said he, "beshrew us both, you know,
But first, beshrew[59] myself, both blood and bones,
If you beguile me, having done so once,
You shall no more, with any flattery,
Cause me to sing and closeup either eye;
610 For he who shuts his eyes when he should see,
And wilfully, God let him ne'er be free!"
"Nay," said the fox, "but God give him mischance[60]
Who is so indiscreet in governance[61]
He chatters when he ought to hold his peace."
615 Lo, such it is when watch and ward do cease,
And one grows negligent with flattery.
But you that hold this tale a foolery,
As but about a fox, a cock, a hen,
Yet do not miss the moral, my good men.
620 For Saint Paul says that all that's written well
Is written down some useful truth to tell.
Then take the wheat and let the chaff lie still.
And now, good God, and if it be Thy will,
As says Lord Christ, so make us all good men
625 And bring us into His high bliss. Amen.

[59]curse

[60]ill fortune

[61]self-control

Glossary and Vocabulary

amain – excessively

amercement – punishment

anon – soon

apothecary – a pharmacist

Aristotle – the ancient Greek philosopher whose work was highly influential in the Middle Ages

aught – any

avarice – greed

aye – ever

behest – to command

"Ben'cite" – "The Lord bless you" (used as an interjection)

bequeath – to bestow property on another by last will

beshrew – to curse

bewray – to reveal

blight – a curse or source of destruction

brazenfacedly – shamelessly

Canterbury – a cathedral in the southeast of England; it was an important destination for Christian pilgrims because it was where Thomas à Becket was murdered.

Catholic Church – the center of religious practices in medieval Europe; churches other than the Catholic church did not come in existence until after 1519, when Martin Luther started the Protestant Reformation. However, some groups of people within the Church did rebel against what they thought were its sinful tendencies. Chaucer himself obviously had some problems with certain trends in the Church, like the selling of indulgences (practiced by The Pardoner) and the "buying off" of Church officials (like The Summoner).

chide – to scold

chivalry – the code of honor among knights, idealized in literature; this code dictated that knights must be honorable, brave, and courteous to women.

churl – a rude man

clergy – the order of religious people divided into *regular* and *secular*; regular clergy included monks and friars, while the secular clergy included local officials like the parson.

contentious – quarrelsome

covetousness – envy

Crusades – a series of wars fought on behalf of the Christian faith; the Crusade at Alexandria is mentioned in connection with The Knight.

cuckold – fool

dalliance – socializing; flirtation

debase – to corrupt or taint

Diana – the Roman goddess of the hunt, wild animals, and fertility

divers – several; various

dotard – a foolish old person

dross – a waste

ere – before

fain – glad, eager

fastidious – critical and hard to please

fay – faith

First Mover – In Aristotelian philosophy, God is the "first cause" of existence; he sets into motion the chain of being that human beings are a part of. Medieval religious philosophy sometimes depicted the universe as a series of circles or spheres, with Earth at the center and God as the "First Mover" at the outside.

frame story – a narrative structure in which one or more stories are contained within another story; the containing story forms a "frame" around the others. Chaucer begins the *Canterbury Tales* with a General Prologue, in which he describes the pilgrims who will each tell a story; their stories then follow, interspersed with details about what happened as they told the stories.

gainsay – to contradict

goodly – large in number; of fine appearance

groat – a silver coin worth four pennies

guilds – trade organizations for artisans and craftsmen, like today's unions; the guilds provided economic and political power for their members. They also purchased public works and entertainment.

heretofore – before now

hie – hurry

humours – fluids within the body that physicians once believed caused ailments when in excess and that resulted in individuals having particular personalities; there are four humors: blood, yellow bile, black bile, and phlegm. People with excess blood were sanguine—happy, passionate, and courageous; those with excess yellow bile were choleric—angry and violent. Individuals with excess black bile were melancholic—irritable and restless, and those with excess phlegm, phlegmatic, were detached and unemotional.

inculcate – to teach; influence

indulgences – the grant of God's grace and forgiveness for money

lecherous – lustful

London – the capital of England and center of trade and commerce; Chaucer knew the city intimately and held positions within the court and London government.

Mars – the Roman god of war

martyr – a person who chooses to die for his or her faith

naught – nothing

niggardly – stingily

nones – occasion

odious – detestable

omnipotent – all powerful

Oxford – the oldest university in England

paramour – a mistress or concubine

pardie – indeed

pennon – a flag or banner

pilgrimage – a journey to a holy site; in Chaucer's time, good Christians were supposed to make a yearly pilgrimage; some of these locations, like Canterbury Cathedral, were places where *martyrs* had died.

pique – to anger or annoy

plague – the disease, also called the Black Death, that wiped out a third of Europe in the fourteenth century

pleasance – pleasure

rancor – hatred and ill-will

reveller – a person who parties all the time

riven – to tear apart

ruth – have mercy

saith – said

sallow – a pussy willow

sapience – good judgment

Saturn – the Roman god of justice, strength, and agriculture

shire – a village

shriven – forgiven

smote – hit

sooth – in truth

sundry – various

swink – to work

Thomas à Becket – the archbishop who was assassinated by royal agents at Canterbury Cathedral and was subsequently made a saint

three estates – the three main divisions of medieval society: the clergy, the aristocracy, and the freemen; in the *Canterbury Tales*, The Knight is the ideal representation of the aristocratic class, while The Parson and The Plowman are the ideal models of the clergy and laboring classes. Of course, as the Wife of Bath illustrates, a person could be born in a somewhat low class and gain both wealth and prestige; the opposite might also occur.

trow – think; suppose; believe

vainglory – pride; vanity

Venus – the Roman goddess of love

verily – in truth; honestly

vernacular – informal, common language as opposed to formal spoken or written language; in the period before Chaucer was born, French was the language spoken by the courts and the upper classes. English was for commoners; because of the war with France, however, the English gained a new sense of national unity, and the English language became more widely spoken.

vestments – clothing

wanton – carefree, reckless

ween – to suppose